Introductory Guide – NHS Governance

A sound and effective governance provides ... supportive environment ... gives an assurance that public ...

Getting governance wrong can ... impact on ... organisation and overall levels of public confidence in the NHS ... must therefore be to develop an effective approach that is not regarded as an unnecessary bureaucratic 'add-on' but rather an intrinsic part of the organisation's DNA, embedded at all levels.

By explaining what governance is and how it works in practice within an NHS organisation, this guide will help your organisation achieve this aim.

Contents

Foreword

This guide has been developed by the HFMA's Governance and Audit Committee and is designed to provide an easy to read but comprehensive introduction to governance in the NHS. It will be an invaluable reference source to anyone with an interest in this area and will be particularly relevant to those involved in establishing and maintaining effective governance structures.

This guide is an updated version of our 2006 publication and takes account of key policy developments in the governance arena since then. It also looks forward to the coalition government's programme of reforms which are in the process of being implemented.

Wherever possible we have included practical examples to help bring the theory to life and to encourage NHS organisations to review their own approach in the light of others' experiences. As in the previous edition, we have retained a summary of 'learning points' at the end of each chapter and supplemented this with a list of key questions that organisations may want to think through to test whether or not their approach to governance is working effectively in practice. There is also an appendix that provides board members with a self assessment tool that they can use to review the health of their organisation's governance framework.

Unfortunately, governance failings continue to emerge in the NHS and elsewhere and these highlight the importance of getting the basics right, whether in terms of sound financial management, effective internal control or adherence to clinical protocols. Development of good governance is the key foundation on which NHS organisations can build so that they are ready to face the challenging times ahead. It is also essential that everyone whatever their role within an organisation understands that they have a part to play in ensuring effective governance – it is not just for the board or leadership team.

Although the guide is based on the governance environment operating in the NHS in England, the underlying principles are common to all, and separate chapters highlight significant differences in Northern Ireland, Scotland and Wales. The text is also structured in such a way that, if readers want to know more about any element of governance, there are pointers to further sources of information.

Committee members have quality assured the guide but inevitably some references will date more quickly than others. There may also be issues that readers feel should be covered in more (or less) detail. As we intend to keep the guide updated on a periodic basis, we would welcome any comments or suggestions to technical.support@hfma.org.uk

John Yarnold,
Chairman,
HFMA Governance and Audit Committee.

Acknowledgements

This guide has been developed by the HFMA's Governance and Audit Committee. The HFMA is grateful to all the committee's members and to their employing organisations for their help and support. The committee's members are:

John Yarnold (Chair)
Paul Baulcombe
Clare Brown
Steve Connor
Derek Corbett
Simon Crick
Ivan Doncaster
Paul Dudfield
Andrew Geldard
Alison Gerrard
Anna Green
David Gregory
John Lappin
David Milner
Alistair Morgan
Paul Moxey
Kemi Oluwole
Val Peacock
Antony Rodden
Phil Rule
Pat Shroff
Michael Townsend
Joanna Watson
Mark Winch.

We are also grateful to Paul Johnson and to John Allen, Linda Devlin, Paula Shearer, Susan Goldsmith, Alan Payne and Steve Elliot who helped update the Northern Ireland, Scotland and Wales chapters.

Chapter 1: What is Governance?

Introduction

Governance has become such a well used term that it is in danger of becoming a cliché, used by everyone but understood by very few. However, a clear understanding of what governance is all about and what makes an effective approach to governance in practice is critical to all organisations across the public, private and voluntary sectors – without this, stakeholders cannot be sure that their interests are being safeguarded, that their organisations are being well managed and that their objectives will be met. For example, without sound governance arrangements, the overriding priority of the NHS – to improve the quality of healthcare – will not be achieved.

This chapter defines governance and looks at the reasons why it remains such a high profile issue across the entire economy.

Definition

The dictionary defines governance as ' the action, manner or system of governing' but it was the use of the phrase 'corporate governance' in the Cadbury Report of 1992, which initiated debate in this area and resulted in a focus on how organisations are run and demonstrate accountability. Corporate governance was defined in the Cadbury Report as 'the system by which companies are directed and controlled'. This direction and control is essentially concerned with the most senior managers/directors within an organisation and how they seek to achieve its objectives and meet the necessary standards of accountability and probity.

In practice this means that governance is all about how an organisation is run – how it structures itself, how it is led and how it is held to account. Cadbury laid down some key principles which have endured through 20 years of updated guidance and good practice:

- governance is concerned with all that an organisation does – not just its administrative and support functions
- organisational culture is a key factor – the principles of good governance must permeate to all levels from the leadership down
- governance is also concerned with structure – the systems, processes and controls that are in place to provide a sound framework for clear and accountable decision-making by senior managers across an organisation
- in terms of leadership, governance is to do with the responsibilities, behaviour and approach of senior managers and with the organisation's underlying culture and values
- as far as accountability is concerned, governance is about both how those running the organisation account for their actions to their stakeholders and how stakeholders can hold them to account.

The enduring nature of the Cadbury definition is supported by the Organisation for Economic Co-operation and Development (OECD) – its 2005 glossary refers to corporate governance as the 'Procedures and processes according to which an organisation is directed and controlled. The corporate governance structure specifies the distribution of rights and responsibilities among the different participants in the organisation – such as the board, managers, shareholders and other stakeholders – and lays down the rules and procedures for decision-making'.

The key point is that governance is not a bureaucratic process that can be carried out periodically. In fact it is not a process at all but rather a matter of structure and attitude, whose aims and principles must underlie all that an organisation does – good governance should be a natural way of life embedded at all levels of an organisation.

Governance in the private sector

Since the Cadbury Report, governance has continued to be a high profile issue across all sectors of the economy. In the private sector, the debate has been fuelled at regular intervals by high-profile scandals and corporate failures, including the collapse of Enron in 2001/02, the world banking crisis in 2008 and BP in 2010.

Many of these organisations appeared, on the face of it, to have governance arrangements in place – including, for example, audit committees. However, it is now clear that these arrangements were not providing the degree of transparency and challenge that they should and that governance was not sufficiently embedded to be effective.

The development of governance principles and practice since Cadbury is interesting, as it shows how the responsibilities placed on those concerned have increased over the years, most notably for executive and non-executive directors (NEDs).

Cadbury itself focused on the financial aspects of corporate governance. As well as defining governance the report identified three fundamental principles:

- openness
- integrity
- accountability.

The report also set out a series of recommendations for public companies, focusing on the roles of boards and directors and mechanisms for reporting and controls. In particular the report emphasised the importance of there being:

- a division of responsibility at the top of an organisation to ensure that there is a balance of power and authority that prevents any one individual having unfettered powers of decision
- a majority of NEDs on the board who are independent of management, able to influence decisions and in a majority on the audit committee
- a public report from the directors on the effectiveness of internal control.

The Combined Code/UK Corporate Governance Code

Following further corporate scandals and concerns about levels of boardroom pay, the Greenbury report (1995) recommended a code of best practice for directors' pay based on accountability, transparency and the linking of rewards to performance. In the same year the Hampel report recommended that companies should include in their annual reports a 'narrative account' of how they apply 14 broad principles of corporate governance.

The Hampel Report (which incorporated the recommendations of both Cadbury and Greenbury) was published by the Financial Services Authority in June 1998 as *The Combined Code on Corporate Governance* which has been mandatory for listed companies since 2000. It requires them to make a two-part disclosure in their annual financial statements covering:

- how the company applies the Code's broad principles
- confirmation that the company complies with the Code's detailed provisions – or the reasons for non-compliance.

As early as 1992, the Cadbury Committee had wanted companies to review and report on the effectiveness of internal control but recognised that established criteria for assessing this did not exist. It therefore called on the accounting profession to come up with some workable criteria and these were issued in the 1999 Turnbull Report (revised in 2005) and led to a requirement on boards to make an annual statement on internal control.

In 2003, a number of studies were commissioned by the former Department of Trade and Industry (now the Department for Business, Innovation and Skills) and these led to the following reports:

- Higgs on the role and effectiveness of NEDs
- Smith on audit committees
- Tyson on the recruitment and development of non-executive directors.

The 2003 version of the *Combined Code* incorporated many of the recommendations in the Higgs and Smith reports and established a new principle – for boards to review their own performance and that of their committees and individual directors.

In March 2009, the FRC announced a further review of the *Combined Code* amidst signs that governance in the UK was about to go through another bout of reform, triggered by the near-collapse of Britain's banking sector in autumn 2008. As the banking crisis unfolded, the spotlight turned from the executives who ran the banks, to the non-executives and investors who owned them, and whether they should have 'challenged' more, particularly in relation to risk and borrowing (referred to as 'leverage'). With hindsight, it appears that there were serious flaws and shortcomings in the system of non-executive oversight of senior management.

While the origins of the banking crisis included low 'real' interest rates, the pursuit of yield, apparent excess liquidity and misplaced trust in financial innovation, the prevailing environment of over-confidence and over-optimism meant that dissenting views and contrary opinion were largely stifled. This led to failure, not only within individual banks, but also in the supervisory system designed to protect the public from systemic risk.

As a result of the crisis the labour government commissioned Sir David Walker to look at governance in the banking sector to ascertain why some banks performed better than others.

His conclusions and recommendations were set out in the 2009 report *Corporate Governance in Banks and Other Financial Industry Entities.*

The FRC's own review of the *Combined Code* took account of the recommendations in the Walker report and led to the publication in 2010 of a revised version of the Code, renamed *The UK Corporate Governance Code.* This Code follows the same 'comply or explain' approach as previous versions and includes four new 'main principles' covering:

- the chairman's responsibility for leading the board
- the non-executive directors' role in challenging and developing strategy
- the need for the board to have a balance of skills, experience, independence and knowledge of the company
- the need for all directors to have sufficient time to discharge their responsibilities effectively.

A full listing of the Code's principles is included at Appendix 2.

Governance in the public sector

Although the governance initiatives mentioned above have tended to focus on the private sector, many of the underlying principles, conclusions and recommendations are equally relevant to public services and many developments have been led or followed by the public sector. For example, in assessing and reporting on internal control, the NHS and other parts of the public sector have led by example.

While there are obvious differences between the public and private sectors, the requirements for good governance have tended to converge over time. One significant difference from a governance point of view is the influence of the Government both in setting objectives for organisations and in prescribing their high level structural and accountability mechanisms (for example, in relation to the board). The focus of governance in most public sector bodies tends therefore to be more on the internal governance of organisations including in particular internal control and risk management. However, it is incumbent on every organisation, board and director to question whether the arrangements laid down actually operate effectively in their case.

The concerns that led to the setting up of the Cadbury Committee and subsequent inquiries were also evident in the public sector with a series of high profile failures in financial stewardship coming to light during the 1980s and 1990s, including those at the Welsh Development Agency, Wessex and West Midlands Regional Health Authorities and Westminster City Council. At the Parliamentary level the 'cash for questions affair' raised concerns relating to the conduct of MPs.

In response to these concerns, the Public Accounts Committee (PAC) issued a landmark report on *The Proper Conduct of Public Business* (1994), as a result of which the Government established the Committee on Standards in Public Life (originally the Nolan Committee). The focus of the initial inquiry was on MPs, ministers, civil servants, 'quangos' and NHS bodies. The Committee reported to the Government in 1995 and identified seven principles of conduct (often referred to as the 'Nolan principles') that should underpin public life:

- selflessness
- integrity
- objectivity
- accountability
- openness
- honesty
- leadership.

The Committee on Standards in Public Life also recommended that:

- all public bodies should draw up codes of conduct incorporating these principles
- internal systems for maintaining standards should be supported by independent scrutiny
- more should be done to promote and reinforce standards in public bodies.

The Committee has since looked at a number of areas in more detail, including:

- the funding of political parties (1998)
- standards of conduct in the House of Lords (2000)
- standards of conduct in the House of Commons (2002)
- relationships between ministers, special advisers and the permanent Civil Service (2003)
- implementing standards of conduct in public life (2005)
- reviewing the Electoral Commission (2007)
- MPs' allowances and expenses (2009)
- party political finance (report due in 2011).

As in the private sector, governance remains high on the agenda for public services. Recent years have seen a range of sector specific initiatives taking forward the Nolan principles and recommendations – for example, codes of practice have been drawn up for central government departments, further and higher education, local government and housing associations; there is a Parliamentary Commissioner for Standards to oversee rules on MPs' interests and public disclosure of donations over £5,000 to political parties is required.

There has also been a concerted effort to develop a common code and set of principles for good governance that could apply across the entire public sector. In 2005 the Independent Commission on Good Governance in Public Services, set up by the Office for Public Management and the Chartered Institute of Public Finance and Accountancy (CIPFA) in partnership with the Joseph Rowntree Foundation, issued its report – the *Good Governance Standard for Public Services*. The Standard comprises six core principles of good governance:

- focusing on the organisation's purpose and on outcomes for citizens and service users
- performing effectively in clearly defined functions and roles
- promoting values for the whole organisation and demonstrating the values of good governance through behaviour
- taking informed, transparent decisions and managing risk
- developing the capacity and capability of the governing body to be effective
- engaging stakeholders and making accountability real.

The Standard also explains what should be done to put these principles into practice and includes a range of good practice examples.

Governance in the NHS

For the NHS, corporate governance was defined by the Audit Commission in its 2003 publication *Corporate Governance: Improvement and Trust in Local Public Services* as 'The framework of accountability to users, stakeholders and the wider community, within which organisations take decisions, and lead and control their functions, to achieve their objectives'.

The health sector has been aware of the importance of good governance for many years with a wide range of separate regulatory frameworks and ethical codes in operation for the different professions working in NHS bodies. The challenge is to bring together the practices and information systems of different disciplines in such a way that together they form an integrated and transparent governance structure. This can then provide NHS boards with assurance over all the activities and services that their organisation provides.

The importance of having sound governance arrangements, high standards and an open culture has been heightened by high profile failures which have arisen over the years and raise questions over the good governance of healthcare services. These include:

- the Bristol Royal Infirmary and Royal Liverpool Children's (Alder Hey) inquiries in 2001
- the Shipman crimes in 2003/04
- the Healthcare Commission's reports into Stoke Mandeville Hospital (2006), Maidstone and Tunbridge Wells NHS Trust (2007) and Mid-Staffordshire NHS Foundation Trust (2009).

In each case the clear linkage drawn between the clinical scandals and the governance failings that allowed them to continue uncorrected has emphasised that effective governance must cover all that an organisation does. It has also driven home to boards just how wide ranging their responsibilities and accountabilities are. In particular, NHS boards must assure themselves that the organisation:

- is providing high quality services in a safe environment – reflecting the fact that 'the primary purpose of the NHS, and everyone working within it, is to provide a high quality service, free at the point of delivery to everyone who needs it'[1]
- has staff that have been appropriately trained
- is engaging with stakeholders, most notably its patients
- is meeting its legal and regulatory requirements
- is meeting its strategic objectives.

Some of the more recent investigations into governance lapses have also underlined the need for governance policies, procedures and structures, as well as board assurance, to be comprehensive and based on intelligent and rigorous scrutiny of processes which may appear

---

[1] *Quality Governance in the NHS – A guide for provider boards,* National Quality Board, 2011.

adequate on paper, but do not operate in practice. For example, the Healthcare Commission's 2009 investigation into Mid-Staffordshire NHS Foundation Trust, (where multiple management failures, led to high mortality rates) found that the Trust, which was seeking to make financial savings in order to apply for foundation trust status, appeared to 'have lost sight of its real priorities'. In relation to standards of care in its emergency services the investigation also found that:

- receptionists performed accident and emergency triage
- just one consultant covered A&E for three months
- minor illness patients prioritised over serious ones to avoid four-hour waiting breaches
- emergency patients left in 'dumping grounds' after admission
- nurses not trained to use cardiac monitors
- patients left in wet or soiled sheets
- surgical patients overseen only by newly qualified doctors at night
- board meetings dominated by finance, targets and foundation status
- deaths deemed to be 'predictable' were not
- some trauma patients left in a 'no man's land' between wards
- resuscitation trolleys unchecked and with out of date medication
- patients left 'nil by mouth' for several days after cancelled operations.

In February 2010 the report by Robert Francis QC on Mid-Staffordshire revealed that deficiencies in staffing and governance extended over a period of more than five years and yet remained un-remedied by those responsible. This report identified a number of basic areas where poor practice had exacerbated the problems and prevented their resolution:

- staffing – shortages of nursing staff went back ten years but staff concerns were not listened to. As a result many staff became disengaged and poor standards became accepted
- outcomes – management relied too much on data and not enough on what patients were saying, too much on systems and not enough on the actual outcomes
- lack of urgency – some problems were identified and actions under way but these did not receive the constant follow-up, review and modification required for them to be effective
- the board – although recognising that the board's role is strategic, Francis says that its members should 'roll their sleeves up' and find out what is happening on the ground, when a bad situation is not getting better.

The Francis Report's comments on the involvement of directors

The Inquiry has had the benefit of hearing the views and thinking of many former and current directors of the Trust. It is clear that many of the problems suffered in this Trust had been in existence for a long time and were known about by those in charge. Many thought – and still think – that they had done their best to address them. While there is no doubt that steps were taken to address many, if not all, of the problems, sadly the action taken was insufficient. I suggest that the board of any trust could benefit from reflecting on their own work in the light of what is described in my report.

> Many of the complaints made to the Inquiry had already been made in precisely the same terms to the Trust. Many of them, even if taken on their own as one person's observation, should have been enough to alert a listener to the existence of a serious systemic problem. Often the responses were formulaic. Even where they were not, the action taken as a result was inadequate. Perhaps most importantly, representative stories hardly ever reached directors.
>
> *Francis report on Mid-Staffordshire Foundation Trust, February 2010.*

Similarly, the Healthcare Commission's investigation in 2006 into the clostridium difficile outbreak at Stoke Mandeville Hospital (in which 354 patients were infected and 33 patients died between October 2003 and June 2005) found that the Trust board was juggling a number of priorities and challenges, including those brought about by recent merger.

These (and other) incidents have served to emphasise just how important it is to see governance arrangements relating to clinical and quality spheres as an integral part of an organisation's overall approach, rather than the preserve of clinicians. The Quality Board's 2011 report makes this clear when it states that 'final and definitive responsibility for improvements, successful delivery, and equally failures, in the quality of care' lie with the provider organisation's board and leaders. It goes on to say that as the 'primary focus of all NHS funded care is to be the delivering of improving quality and outcomes, the distinction between quality governance and clinical governance is less relevant as clinicians and managers are working towards the same ends – the delivery of the highest quality services.'

The Audit Commission's 2009 report *Taking it on Trust – a review of how NHS trusts and foundation trusts get their assurance* also emphasised the importance of an organisation wide approach to governance when it suggested that future failures were likely unless a systematic approach is taken to identifying and managing key risks, and to evaluating assurances.

This focus on risk and assurance across all that an organisation does is a key part of an integrated approach to governance which has been gaining ground in the NHS since the early 1990s. Before then governance had tended to develop in a piecemeal fashion, focusing either on clinical, financial or organisational aspects with a particular focus on non-clinical systems and processes that were considered easier to measure, assess and adapt.

The key developments in the growth of integrated governance include initiatives such as:

- the development of codes of conduct and accountability (see chapters 3 and 5)
- the publication of a code of practice on openness (see chapter 3)
- guidance for accountable officers (see chapter 5)
- the requirement for all NHS bodies to include a statement on internal control (SIC) in their financial statements (see chapters 6 and 7)
- the code of conduct for NHS managers (see chapter 3)
- the publication of *Governing the NHS: a Guide for NHS Boards* (see chapter 5)
- the development of a board assurance framework (see chapter 7)

- the development of internal audit and the introduction of standards (see chapter 7)
- guidance on audit committees, including the handbook (see chapter 5)
- the publication of guidance on integrated governance (see chapters 2 and 5)
- model standing orders, schemes of delegation and reservation of powers and standing financial instructions (see chapter 6)
- the development of the *NHS Constitution* (see chapter 3)
- the publication of *Quality Governance in the NHS* (see chapter 8).

Of particular relevance in practical terms was the publication by the Department of Health in 2006 of the *Integrated Governance Handbook*, which emphasised the importance of pulling together 'all the competing pressures on boards and their supporting structures, to enable good governance'. In particular, the Handbook identified eight key questions that boards should ask themselves, to ensure that the organisation's strategic direction, assurance framework and high-level governance framework are consistent with one another:

	Governance Framework	Illustrative Question
1.	Resources	Are we financially sustainable to deliver on this objective?
2.	4 Es (effectiveness, efficiency, economy and efficacy)	Are the systems effective, efficient and economic, and have we challenged the appropriateness of our delivery of the service?
3.	Compliance with authorisations	Can we be sure we are compliant in our delivery of the service at all times with competing authorisations?
4.	Compliance with Standards for Better Health [since superseded by CQC regime]	Will we be compliant with the Department of Health's Standards for Better Health? [now the CQC's standards]
5.	The duty of quality	Are our systems supporting and encouraging improvements in clinical quality?
6.	The duty of partnership	Are we using the information to communicate with stakeholders in our community?
7.	The duty of patient and public involvement, in particular, in the planning of services	Have we involved the patients and public in decisions about their care by demonstrating the effectiveness of various clinical options?
8.	The ongoing development of the board	Does the board understand the issue, and the relevance, of reliable clinical or non-clinical information systems?

In 2007, the guidance set out in the Handbook was developed further in an HFMA publication called *Integrated Governance: Delivering Reform on Two and a Half Days a Month*. This guide was aimed primarily at NHS board members and provided practical pointers about developing an integrated approach to governance. It focused on board behaviours, structures and systems and looked at ways in which boards could put in place supports that would give them the assurances they needed. A revised and updated version of this Guide was released in 2011 re-titled *Integrated Governance: a guide to risk and joining up the NHS reforms*.

Key questions for the organisation to consider

1. Do we cover governance and its importance in our induction programme – at all levels?
2. Does this include awareness of the three key principles of good governance?
3. Is everyone aware of the Nolan principles – do they adhere to them?
4. Does everyone understand what the organisation's primary purpose is – to provide a high quality sustainable service?
5. Do our board members appreciate how wide ranging their responsibilities are?
6. Do we as an organisation understand what governance is and why an integrated approach across all activities is important?
7. Do board members consider that they and the organisation generally comply with the principles of good governance?
8. If so, what sources of evidence do we have to support this belief? If we are unsure what do we need to do?
9. Does the organisation have systems in place to ensure that it is aware of lessons from governance failures both in the public and private sectors and are lessons learned/ actions taken as a result?

This chapter's main learning points

- Governance (or 'corporate governance') is the system by which organisations are directed and controlled
- There are three fundamental principles of good governance – openness, integrity and accountability
- Good governance, which involves a continual assessment of fitness for purpose, is critical to the effectiveness of all organisations – whatever sector they operate in
- Good governance should underpin all that an organisation does – in the NHS this means it must be an integrated approach encompassing clinical, financial and organisational aspects
- Governance policies, procedures and structures must be comprehensive, and based on intelligent and rigorous scrutiny of processes
- Governance failures are likely unless a systematic approach is taken to identifying and managing key risks
- Organisations must learn from their own and other organisations' governance failures
- There are clear linkages between clinical scandals and governance failings
- Boards' responsibilities are wide ranging and they must bear in mind at all times that the primary purpose is to provide high quality healthcare
- There will always be policy developments and topical issues affecting governance and putting strain on governance structures

- Organisations need to be open about the impact of change and have mechanisms that allow discussion and communication so that an effective response is possible
- In times of change the basic control framework needs to be maintained, not least to provide a secure platform for development
- An effective governance framework is essential if organisations are to cope with change and thrive.

Further reading

The Report of the Committee on the Financial Aspects of Corporate Governance (The Cadbury Report) December, 1992

The Greenbury Report, 1995

The Hampel Report, 1998 – The Combined Code on Corporate Governance

Internal Control: Guidance for Directors on the Combined Code (The Turnbull Report), 1999

The Higgs Report on the Role and Effectiveness of NEDs, 2003

Audit Committees – Combined Code Governance (The Smith Report), 2003

The Tyson Report on the Recruitment and Development of NEDs, 2003

All of the above are available at:
www.icaew.com/en/library/subject-gateways/corporate-governance/codes-and-reports

Corporate Governance in Banks and Other Financial Industry Entities, 2009:
www.hm-treasury.gov.uk/d/walker_review_261109.pdf

Proper Conduct of Public Business: Eighth Report of 1993-94 from the Committee of Public Accounts, HMSO, 1994
www.parliament.uk/parliamentary_committees/committee_of_public_accounts.cfm

The UK Corporate Governance Code, Financial Reporting Council, 2010:
www.frc.org.uk/corporate/ukcgcode.cfm

The Good Governance Standard for Public Services, the Independent Commission on Good Governance in Public Services, OPM and CIPFA, 2004:
www.opm.co.uk
www.cipfa.org.uk/panels/corporate_governance/publications.cfm

Corporate Governance: Improvement and Trust in Local Public Services, Audit Commission, 2003:
www.audit-commission.gov.uk

Quality Governance in the NHS, Department of Health, 2011:
www.dh.gov.uk/en/Publicationsandstatistics/Publications/PublicationsPolicyAndGuidance/DH_125238

Robert Francis Inquiry Report into Mid-Staffordshire NHS Foundation Trust, 2010:
www.dh.gov.uk/en/Publicationsandstatistics/Publications/PublicationsPolicyAndGuidance/DH_113018

Helping the NHS put patients at the heart of care, Department of Health, 2009:
www.dh.gov.uk/en/Publicationsandstatistics/Publications/PublicationsPolicyAndGuidance/DH_106046

Taking it on Trust: A Review of how Boards of NHS Trusts and NHS Foundation Trusts get their Assurance, Audit Commission, 2009:
www.audit-commission.gov.uk

The Integrated Governance Handbook, Department of Health, 2006:
www.dh.gov.uk/en/Publicationsandstatistics/Publications/PublicationsPolicyAndGuidance/DH_4128739

Integrated Governance: a guide to risk and joining up the NHS reforms, HFMA, 2011:
www.hfma.org.uk/publications-and-guidance/publicationitem.htm?publicationid=46&catid=2

Chapter 2: How the Elements of Governance fit together in the NHS

Introduction

Good governance underpins all of an organisation's activities and consists of a number of different elements. It is also reflected in the organisational style, culture and tone – aspects that are often regarded as less important. This chapter looks at why the focus on effective governance is important in the NHS and explains how the different constituent parts fit together to form a cohesive and coherent whole.

Why is good governance important in the NHS?

As well as establishing a safe and supportive environment within which high quality healthcare can be delivered and the organisation's objectives achieved, good governance provides an assurance to stakeholders that:

- things are running as they should
- public money is being used correctly and well
- accountabilities and responsibilities are clear
- there is a culture of openness
- there are high standards of professional, managerial and personal conduct.

The shortcomings and public inquiries mentioned in chapter 1 make clear why good governance is so important – if an NHS organisation gets it wrong it can have a catastrophic impact on patients and undermine public confidence in the service as a whole. This history of governance breakdowns in the NHS also explains why there is a need for all organisations (both established and newly emerging) to ensure that they have in place an effective and comprehensive approach to governance that is constantly reviewed and improved. In particular, organisations must focus on how they:

- are led and structured
- demonstrate that they are operating in line with the fundamental principles – openness, integrity and accountability
- are going about meeting the statutory objective of providing high quality healthcare
- ensure that they operate economically, efficiently and effectively.

In some organisations there is a tendency to assume that governance will somehow take care of itself or is someone else's responsibility. This view prevailed early on in the development of NHS governance when attention tended to focus disproportionately on putting in place detailed control frameworks rather than looking at the impact of wider, harder to measure elements such as clinical effectiveness, service quality and the importance of good leadership. Whilst this emphasis helped organisations get to grips with governance and to verify and improve their systems, it also tended to confirm the view that governance was essentially a bureaucratic process undertaken for the benefit of others. This is a mistake: good governance is not a discretionary 'add-on' or a series of independent tasks that can be ticked off a list and forgotten about. Rather governance must be viewed as a continuous, organisation-wide activity that is essential to the health, effectiveness and reputation of an organisation and which involves everyone in an organisation.

The fact that governance must not be seen as an end in itself but should instead contribute to and support the organisation's overall aims and objectives is made clear in the NHS Appointments Commission's 2003 guide *Governing the NHS: a Guide for NHS Boards*, which emphasises in its introduction that:

> '…each board's prime duty is to ensure good governance. Achieving high standards of patient care depends on it. The protection of patients, staff and the wider public depends on it. Accountability for the proper use of unprecedented amounts of public money depends on it. And, critically, good governance arrangements ensure that front line teams have the appropriate protection and space within agreed rules to learn from failures as well as successes'.

The *Integrated Governance Handbook* also stresses that good governance depends on there being an approach that 'spans the various functional governance processes that are often unlinked and result in the handling of issues in silos'.

More recently, the Audit Commission's 2009 report *Taking it on Trust* reinforces the importance of treating governance as a 'living' activity when it emphasises that the key is not simply having governance structures and processes in place, but rather looking at the rigour with which they operate and provide boards with the assurances they need.

The impact of poor governance

It is essential that organisations do not take the view that a failure in governance 'could never happen here'. Things can and do go wrong in all types of organisation and problems are more likely to arise if there is a complacent attitude or denial. This does not relate only to failures in finance or service provision. Most organisations now have systems to prevent or detect significant failures but these too can go wrong and good governance means the provision of regular assurance to the board that these arrangements are working effectively. This should include details of significant risks or incidents that have been identified and updates on actions taken to put them right or prevent a recurrence.

Examples of inadequate corporate governance could scarcely be more dramatic than the sudden collapse of Enron in 2001/02 which revealed the failure of internal control and accountancy malpractice and dented the confidence of investors around the world. Although reforms were introduced after those failures they did not prevent the banking crisis which unfolded from 2007/08, suggesting that more attention needs to be given to the behavioural and cultural (rather than procedural) aspects of governance. The best-constituted board in the world counts for nothing unless its debates and decision-making are sound and based on effective and robust challenge.

NHS boards may be tempted to think that these incidents are not relevant to them but that would be foolhardy – the public inquiries mentioned in chapter 1 all identified important lessons that apply across the NHS. And there are many others – for example, in 2002, financial failings were uncovered at Bedfordshire Shared Services – here, the controls that should have operated in relation to the core financial systems failed, resulting in:

- a breakdown in financial control
- an increased risk of undetected fraud, corruption and error
- inadequate financial reporting
- the risk of inaccurate financial data, which cannot be relied upon for preparing the annual accounts.[1]

On the clinical side, the 2001 inquiry into the treatment of very sick children at the Bristol Royal Infirmary found a number of significant governance failings including:

- unsafe arrangements for caring for the children
- no requirement for consultants to keep their skills and knowledge up to date
- no agreed standards of care
- no openness about clinical performance
- no systematic mechanism for monitoring the clinical performance of healthcare professionals or hospitals.

Further scandals at North Yorkshire and the West Midlands regional health authorities in the 1990s, the Alder Hey Children's Hospital (2001) and Shipman (2005) inquiries and the independent report into financial problems at North Bristol NHS Trust (2003) all raised concerns about governance.

More recently, the 2007 Healthcare Commission investigation into Maidstone and Tunbridge Wells NHS Trust found that between April 2004 and September 2006, clostridium difficile was probably or definitely the main cause of death for 90 patients; was definitely a contributing factor in the deaths of a further 124, and a probable factor in another 55 deaths. The Commission's report highlighted the fact that reconfiguring services, opening an independent sector treatment centre, managing a financial deficit, as well as applying for foundation trust status had all contributed to the trust 'taking its collective eye off the clinical ball'. It also cited the following concerns:

- change in the structure and responsibilities relating to governance, leading to confusion over accountability
- matters requiring consideration and resolution at a strategic level were rarely considered by the board, whether as a whole board, or at its governance or risk sub-committees
- no systematic mechanism to follow up any actions required or to share lessons
- the risk register and assurance framework were not well understood
- the record of attendance by clinical directors at the various governance and risk committees was poor, and the committees did not monitor or give adequate leadership and support to the directorates.

---

[1] Public Interest Report, May 2002.

In all these examples, controls systems failed to highlight problems at an early stage with disastrous consequences.

The governance framework

This guide has referred several times to the importance of having a sound 'framework' of governance that underpins everything an organisation does and that should help prevent such dramatic failings. But what does this mean in practice – what is a framework of governance?

In simple terms it is to do with establishing an integrated approach to governance that translates the three fundamental principles of openness, integrity and accountability into a working model that applies across all activities. It may help to view governance as a series of interrelated cogs in a machine – all the cogs need to work smoothly to produce the end product.

The different cogs are all important in their own right but they only make sense when they are all in place at the same time and working towards the same ends. For example:

- budgetary control is ineffective unless action is taken to reduce overspends when they are highlighted
- there is no point to clinical incident reporting unless action is planned to prevent further incidents and plans are followed up to ensure they are implemented and effective
- performance reporting is ineffective unless the data it is based on is reliable and up to date
- non-executive directors who accept management assertions are ineffective unless they challenge and seek positive assurance that reports are reliable, problems identified are addressed and remedial action planned is carried out.

At the same time it is important to recognise that no framework of governance, however sophisticated, can guarantee that there will be no management or clinical failures or fraudulent behaviour. What it can do is provide an assurance that systems and processes are in place to minimise the possibility of corporate failures and identify any potential problems at an early stage, encouraging management to manage effectively.

If a breakdown in governance does occur, there should be a process for recovery which is far more likely to be effective if an organisation:

- establishes the full facts (not opinions) as soon as possible and from as wide a range of sources as possible
- does not look to attribute blame at an early stage
- gets to the root cause of the breakdown rather than treating the symptoms. For example, if goods have not been tendered for, is it due to lack of knowledge of procedures, lack of time from too much work and too little support, or a deliberate breach by a maverick employee?

The elements of governance

The NHS is an extremely complex and complicated set of organisations so any guide – including this one – will inevitably simplify matters. However, to help make sense of the

governance agenda, each of three key elements is discussed in succeeding chapters of this guide – namely:

- culture and values ('people' issues)
    - organisational 'tone', culture, behaviour and leadership (chapter 3)
    - public sector values/codes of conduct (chapter 3)
- organisational policies, structures and processes
    - the external environment – political and regulatory requirements (chapter 4)
    - organisational structures – how an NHS organisation is run (chapter 5)
    - detailed statutory requirements (chapter 6)
    - foundation trusts (chapter 9)
- control frameworks
    - risk management and assurance (chapter 7)
    - internal and external audit (chapter 7)
    - clinical governance (chapter 8).

Key questions for the organisation to consider

1. What is our organisational 'tone'? Is it what we want it to be? How is it set?
2. Is everyone clear about the organisation's purpose?
3. Is the organisation's structure clear and coherent?
4. Do we understand how the structure fits together?
5. Do we understand how the organisation fits into the overall structure of the NHS?
6. Do all staff understand who is responsible for what within the overall organisational structure?
7. Do all staff understand that they have a role to play in governance terms?
8. Does the board understand that it is ultimately responsible for ensuring good governance?
9. Do we continually review our governance structures and processes?
10. Is there sufficient openness at all levels?
11. Is there sufficient challenge at all levels but in particular, from executive directors to managers; between executive directors; between board members?
12. What is our process for recovery if a governance breakdown occurs?

This chapter's main learning points

- Good governance will not take care of itself – it is a priority and essential to the health, effectiveness and reputation of an organisation
- Governance failings can happen anywhere and can be dramatic – there is no room for complacency
- The governance framework covers culture and values, organisational policies, structures and processes and control frameworks – it is more than the sum of its parts
- No framework of governance can guarantee absolutely that there will be no failures

- A good governance framework minimises the risk of problems, and provides assurances to stakeholders that things are as they should be
- It is important to have in place a process for recovery that can be followed if a governance breakdown occurs.

Further reading

Governing the NHS: A Guide for NHS Boards, NHS Appointments Commission and Department of Health, 2003:
www.dh.gov.uk/PublicationsAndStatistics/Publications/PublicationsPolicyAndGuidance/fs/en

The Integrated Governance Handbook, Department of Health, 2006:
www.dh.gov.uk/en/Publicationsandstatistics/Publications/PublicationsPolicyAndGuidance/DH_4128739

Taking it on Trust: A Review of how Boards of NHS Trusts and NHS Foundation Trusts get their Assurance, Audit Commission, 2009:
www.audit-commission.gov.uk

Inquiry into the Management of Care of Children Receiving Complex Heart Surgery at the Bristol Royal Infirmary: www.bristol-inquiry.org.uk

The Royal Liverpool Children's Inquiry (Alder Hey): www.rlcinquiry.org.uk/

The Shipman Inquiry: www.the-shipman-inquiry.org.uk/

Public Interest Reports – details available from the Audit Commission's website:
www.audit-commission.gov.uk

Investigation into outbreaks of clostridium difficile at Maidstone and Tunbridge Wells NHS Trust – Healthcare Commission, 2007: www.cqc.org.uk/_db/_documents/Maidstone_and_Tunbridge_Wells_investigation_report_Oct_2007.pdf

Investigation into Mid Staffordshire NHS Foundation Trust, Healthcare Commission, 2009: www.cqc.org.uk/_db/_documents/Investigation_into_Mid_Staffordshire_NHS_Foundation_Trust.pdf

Chapter 3: Public Sector Values and Organisational Culture

Introduction

Chapter one emphasised that governance is as much about behaviour, values and attitudes as about structures, systems and processes. There is no point having a comprehensive governance framework if no-one is committed to it or understands why it exists and what it is designed to achieve. Often these 'softer' issues are regarded as less important but this is a mistake: it is essential that an organisation invests time and effort in developing a 'tone' and culture that is in tune with the principles of good governance.

This chapter looks at organisational culture and values and identifies key sources of guidance and support that are relevant to the NHS, including Nolan's seven principles, the codes of conduct, accountability and openness and the *NHS Constitution*.

Organisational values and culture

The *Good Governance Standard for Public Services* recognises that 'Good governance flows from a shared ethos or culture' and that it is 'the governing body that should take the lead in establishing and promoting values for the organisation and its staff'. In other words, the culture and values of an organisation are set from the top. In the context of the NHS this means that the behaviour, approach and leadership style of the board and senior management are critical in establishing an organisation's tone, 'feel' and direction.

Example of a board leading on culture

Cardiff and Vale UHB have held 'Patient Safety Fridays' since 2009 based on an approach used in a New York hospital. This involves board members spending Friday mornings focussing on improving patient safety by meeting frontline staff in an effort 'to understand more about what the UHB does to keep patients safe, and what it needs to do better.'

Each WalkRound involves at least two board members (usually one is a NED and one an executive director) accompanied by a 'scribe' to take a record of the discussions and write a report following the visit. WalkRound groups are no larger than four to keep disruption to a minimum.

The focus is on patient safety and the UHB's own quality and safety priorities (for example, reducing healthcare associated infections; venous thromboembolism risk assessment and inpatient falls). This focus is used to inform discussions and reinforce key messages about the importance the board attaches to the patient safety and quality agenda.

As well as the actual board member discussions with frontline staff, an important part of the process is for the executives to follow up on concerns that are raised, and this feeds into the board's 'You said, we did' staff engagement campaign.

A report of the discussions is written, shared with those involved to agree accuracy and actions, and then forwarded to the divisional management teams and the executive directors (and their assistant directors) for action. Executive action updates are provided at the bi-monthly quality and safety committee and local actions through the quality and safety divisional group.

In addition to hearing concerns about safety and quality, the WalkRounds are used to visit areas of excellence, for board members to see how services have overcome barriers to improve safety and quality.

Every organisation develops its own unique culture and values but to be effective, it is essential that there is 'a system of shared values and beliefs about what is important, what behaviours are appropriate and about feelings and relationships internally and externally'.[1] If everyone within an organisation is to 'buy in' to these shared values they must be meaningful, make sense and be realistic. There is no point having a carefully crafted statement of values if it bears no relation to how things actually feel on the front line. For example there is no point in an organisation claiming it has a 'no blame culture' if this is not borne out in practice.

Example of a vision and values statement

North Essex Partnership NHS Foundation Trust

'OUTSTANDING CARE TRANSFORMING LIVES'

Our vision is to provide care that is outstanding in its quality, transforming the lives of individuals and families every day. Our communities will have total confidence in our services, our staff feel a strong sense of belonging and satisfaction, and our partners be proud to work purposefully with us.

Our commitments:

To individuals and families:

- we will work together, building on strengths, to improve mental health and wellbeing.

To our staff:

- we will value everyone individually, promote wellbeing, support involvement and encourage personal development and leadership
- we will support teams in their delivery of best value, innovation and excellence.

---

[1] *Vision and Values: organisational culture and values as a source of competitive advantage*, CIPD, 2004: www.cipd.co.uk

To our commissioners and key partners:

- we will listen, work with you, create ideas, demonstrate our effectiveness and flexibility, and earn recognition as provider of choice.

Our values underpin everything we do:

- promoting dignity, respect and compassion
- demonstrating openness, honesty and integrity
- building on individual strengths
- tackling stigma, promoting inclusion and valuing diversity
- listening, learning, and continuously improving to deliver quality and value.

Principles of public life

Everyone involved in the public sector brings their own personality, experience and behaviour with them. However, the public provides the resources for which they are responsible and, as a result, certain ethical standards and values are expected of them.

These standards were set out most clearly in the Nolan Committee's *Seven Principles of Public Life*:[2]

- **selflessness** – holders of public office should take decisions solely in terms of the public interest. They should not do so in order to gain financial or other material benefits for themselves, their family, or their friends
- **integrity** – holders of public office should not place themselves under any financial or other obligation to outside individuals or organisations that might influence them in the performance of their official duties
- **objectivity** – in carrying out public business, including making public appointments, awarding contracts, or recommending individuals for rewards and benefits, holders of public office should make choices on merit
- **accountability** – holders of public office are accountable for their decisions and actions to the public and must submit to whatever scrutiny is appropriate to their office
- **openness** – holders of public office should be as open as possible about all the decisions and actions that they take. They should give reasons for their decisions and restrict information only when the wider public interest clearly demands it
- **honesty** – holders of public office have a duty to declare any private interests relating to their public duties and to take steps to resolve any conflicts arising in a way that protects the public interest
- **leadership** – holders of public office should promote and support these principles by leadership and example.

---

[2] *First report of The Committee on Standards in Public Life*, May 1995. www.public-standards.gov.uk

The Treasury's guidance document, *Managing Public Money* also sets out the standards which it expects all public services to deliver which overlap with the Nolan principles:

- honesty
- fairness
- impartiality
- integrity
- openness
- transparency
- accountability
- objectivity
- accuracy
- reliability.

However, the Treasury adds that organisations should carry them out:

- 'In the spirit of, as well as to the letter of, the law
- in the public interest
- to high ethical standards
- achieving value for money.'

Together, the Nolan principles and Treasury standards provide a blueprint for the underlying culture and values of any public sector organisation.

The NHS Constitution

The *NHS Constitution* further emphasises the importance of having clear (and consistently applied) principles underpinning all that the NHS does. Since January 2010 all providers and commissioners of NHS care have a statutory duty to have regard to the *NHS Constitution* in all their decisions and actions. As the Department of Health's website states: 'This means that the Constitution, its pledges, principles, values and responsibilities need to be fully embedded and ingrained into everything the NHS does.'

The Constitution builds on the overarching objectives and values first set out in 2000 in *The NHS Plan, A Plan for Investment, A Plan for Reform*, namely that:

- the NHS will provide a universal service for all based on clinical need, not ability to pay
- the NHS will provide a comprehensive range of services
- the NHS will shape its services around the needs and preferences of individual patients, their families and their carers
- the NHS will respond to different needs of different populations
- the NHS will work continuously to improve quality services and to minimise errors
- the NHS will support and value its staff
- public funds for healthcare will be devoted solely to NHS patients
- the NHS will work together with others to ensure a seamless service for patients
- the NHS will help keep people healthy and work to reduce health inequalities
- the NHS will respect the confidentiality of individual patients and provide open access to information about services, treatment and performance.

Of particular note in governance terms are the principles and values set out in the Constitution as these need to underpin everything that an organisation does.

NHS Constitution – seven principles

- the NHS provides a comprehensive service, available to all
- access to NHS services is based on clinical need, not an individual's ability to pay
- the NHS aspires to the highest standards of excellence and professionalism
- NHS services must reflect the needs and preferences of patients, their families and carers
- the NHS works across organisational boundaries and in partnership with other organisations in the interests of patients, local communities and the wider population
- the NHS is committed to providing best value for taxpayers' money and the most effective, fair and sustainable use of finite resources
- the NHS is accountable to the public, communities and patients that it serves.

NHS Constitution – values

- respect and dignity – respecting each person as an individual and seeking to understand their priorities, needs, abilities and limits
- commitment to quality of care – striving to get the basics right every time: safety, confidentiality, professional and managerial integrity, accountability, dependable service and good communication
- compassion – responding with humanity to each person's pain, distress, anxiety or need
- improving lives – striving to improve health and well-being and people's experiences of the NHS
- working together for patients – putting the needs of patients, carers, families and communities before organisational boundaries
- everyone counts – using resources for the benefit of the whole community, ensuring nobody is excluded or left behind and accepting that some people need more help.

The Constitution puts stakeholders, most notably patients, at the centre of decision-making and accountability. Boards therefore need to consider how they can understand, monitor and review the impact of the *NHS Constitution* for patients, public and staff. This will involve using data from, for example, staff and patient surveys, records of complaints, and feedback from patients and their representatives including Patient Advocacy and Liaison Services (PALs) and Local Involvement Networks (local HealthWatch once the government's reforms are implemented).

The coalition government has made clear that it will 'uphold and reinforce the *NHS Constitution*, which all providers and commissioners will be obliged to have regard to in carrying out their functions.' This means that in the future, new NHS organisations (including clinical commissioning groups) will continue to have a legal responsibility 'to have regard' to the *NHS Constitution* in all that they do.

NHS codes of practice

As long ago as 1994, the NHS published the first of four codes of behaviour which NHS organisations are still required to follow. They cover:

- conduct
- accountability
- openness.

The Department of Health's *Integrated Governance Handbook* also includes guidance on board etiquette and best practice approaches. For foundation trusts (FTs), best practice guidance is included in Monitor's *NHS Foundation Trust Code of Governance* which is based on the private sector *UK Corporate Governance Code* (see chapter 1) and applies on a 'comply or explain' basis.

It is not yet clear which of these codes will be relevant once the coalition government's planned changes are introduced. However, as the principles they set down will remain equally relevant each is summarised below.

Code of Conduct for NHS Boards

The *Code of Conduct for NHS Boards* was first issued jointly by the Department of Health and the NHS Appointments Commission in April 1994, and revised in 2002 and 2004. The key message is that three crucial public sector values must be at the heart of the NHS:

- '**Accountability** – everything done by those who work in the NHS must be able to stand the test of Parliamentary scrutiny, public judgements on propriety and professional codes of conduct
- **probity** – there should be an absolute standard of honesty in dealing with the assets of the NHS: integrity should be the hallmark of all personal conduct in decisions affecting patients, staff and suppliers, and in the use of information acquired in the course of NHS duties
- **openness** – there should be sufficient transparency about NHS activities to promote confidence between the NHS organisation and its staff, patients and the public.'

All board directors are required to subscribe to the Code and 'satisfy themselves that the actions of the board and its directors in conducting board business fully reflect the values in this Code and, as far as is reasonably practicable, that concerns expressed by staff or others are fully investigated and acted upon.'

The Code emphasises that its success 'depends on a vigorous and visible example from boards and the consequential influence on the behaviour of all those who work within the organisation. Boards have a clear responsibility for corporate standards of conduct and acceptance of the Code should inform and govern the decisions and conduct of all board directors'.

The Code is brief (only 4 pages) but covers a number of key issues:

- public service values
- general principles
- openness and public responsibilities

- public service values in management
- public business and private gain
- hospitality and other expenditure
- relations with suppliers
- staff
- compliance.

For FTs, the relevant guidance in this area is *The Code of Governance* issued by Monitor, which again builds on the principles and provisions of the *UK Corporate Governance Code* (see chapter 1). This contains a 'supporting principle' that relates to the conduct of boards which states that 'the board of directors should set the NHS foundation trust's values and standards of conduct and ensure that its obligations to its members, patients and other stakeholders are understood and met'. This principle is translated into 'code provisions' A.1.9 and A.1.10:

'The board of directors should establish the values and standards of conduct for the NHS foundation trust and its staff in accordance with NHS values and accepted standards of behaviour in public life, which include the principles of selflessness, integrity, objectivity, accountability, openness, honesty and leadership (the Nolan principles).'

'The board of directors should operate a code of conduct that builds on the values of the NHS foundation trust and reflect high standards of probity and responsibility. The board of directors should follow a policy of openness and transparency in its proceedings and decision making unless this conflicts with a need to protect the wider interests of the public or the NHS foundation trust (including commercial-in-confidence matters) and make clear how potential conflicts of interest are dealt with.'

Code of Accountability for NHS Boards

The *Code of Accountability for NHS Boards* was published alongside the *Code of Conduct for NHS Boards*, and was also revised in 2004. This Code defines the statutory duties of NHS boards and accountability regimes to the Secretary of State. It is another succinct document that includes sections on:

- status
- code of conduct
- statutory accountability
- the board of directors
- the role of the chair
- non-executive directors
- reporting and controls
- declaration of interests
- employee relations.

The Department of Health and the NHS Appointments Commission also published more detailed guidance for boards including *Governing the NHS: a Guide for NHS Boards* which emphasises that each board's prime duty is to ensure good governance. It sets out how this should be achieved in the NHS and stressed that 'Non-executive directors are appointed by the

NHS Appointments Commission on behalf of the local community. They therefore have a responsibility to ensure the board acts in the best interests of the public and is fully accountable to the public for the services provided by the organisation and the public funds it uses'.[3]

The accountability regime for FTs is set out in Monitor's *Code of Governance* – see chapter 9 for more details.

Code of Practice on Openness in the NHS

The latest version of the Department of Health's *Code of Practice on Openness in the NHS* was issued in 2003 and reflected changes in legislation relating to human rights, freedom of information and data protection. The aims of the Code are 'to ensure that people:

- have access to available information about the services provided by the NHS, the cost of those services, quality standards and performance against targets
- are provided with explanations about proposed service changes and have an opportunity to influence decisions on such changes
- are aware of the reasons for decisions and actions affecting their own treatment
- know what information is available and where they can get it.'

The basic principle of the Code is that the NHS should respond positively to requests for information except in circumstances set out in the Code – for example the need to keep patients' records safe and confidential.

The Code applies to 'health authorities, special health authorities, NHS trusts, PCTs, the Mental Health Act Commission (since subsumed within the Care Quality Commission), community health councils (since abolished in England), family doctors, dentists, optometrists, opticians and community pharmacists', with specific requirements for most of these organisations detailed in separate annexes. Organisations not covered in the annexes are required to apply the general principles of the Code in their dealings with the public.

As well as setting out the basic principles that must be adhered to, the Code gives detailed guidance on:

- information that must be provided and that which can be withheld
- how to respond to requests for information
- circumstances when charges can be made for providing information
- handling complaints.

Although this Code does not apply to FTs, Monitor's *Code of Governance* states that 'the board of directors should follow a policy of openness and transparency in its proceedings and decision making...'[4]

---

[3] Under the coalition government's planned changes, the Appointments Commission will cease to exist and NED appointments will be made by the Department of Health.

[4] *The NHS Foundation Trust Code of Governance*, provision A.1.10

More recently, the Department of Health has emphasised the importance of protecting sensitive patient information, particularly during a time of structural change. A toolkit on NHS information governance is available to help organisations fulfil their responsibilities in this area.[5]

Code of Conduct for NHS Managers

The *Code of Conduct for NHS Managers* was published in October 2002 and was drawn up following a recommendation in the Kennedy report into the management of care of children receiving complex heart surgery at the Bristol Royal Infirmary. This Code sets out the core standards of conduct expected of NHS managers and is designed to serve two purposes:

- to guide NHS managers and employing health bodies in the work they do and the decisions and choices they have to make
- to reassure the public that these important decisions are being made against a background of professional standards and accountability.

Code of Conduct for NHS Managers – the six core standards

- make the care and safety of patients the first concern and act to protect them from risk
- respect the public, patients, relatives, carers, NHS staff and partners in other agencies
- be honest and act with integrity
- accept responsibility for their own work and the proper performance of the people they manage
- show commitment to working as a team member by working with all NHS colleagues and the wider community
- take responsibility for personal learning and development.

Enforcement of Codes of Practice – example approaches

NHS organisations use a variety of approaches to try and ensure that staff are aware of relevant codes of practice and adhere to them. Examples include:

- covering codes of conduct in induction programmes
- issuing codes to all staff and requiring return of a tear off slip confirming receipt; that the code has been read and understood and that it will be complied with
- producing short guides to governance that identify staff roles and responsibilities
- audits to assess levels of awareness and compliance
- regular emails to staff highlighting examples of good (and bad) governance and the part they can play
- conducting regular staff surveys.

---

[5] Information governance toolkit: www.igt.connectingforhealth.nhs.uk/about.aspx

Professional codes of practice

As well as specific NHS codes of practice, many professional bodies on both the clinical and managerial side have their own codes of conduct and disciplinary regimes that apply to their members.

Leadership

Good leadership and management are crucial both to good governance and to the overall vision and effectiveness of an organisation. Of particular relevance to the NHS is the 'leadership qualities framework' developed in 2005 by the NHS Institute for Innovation and Improvement. This framework identifies the 'key characteristics, attitudes and behaviours to which leaders should aspire'. There are fifteen qualities split into three groups:

- personal qualities: self belief; self awareness; self management; drive for improvement; personal integrity
- setting direction: broad scanning; intellectual flexibility; seizing the future; political astuteness; drive for results
- delivering the service: leading change through people; holding to account; empowering others; effective and strategic influencing; collaborative working.

There is also an assessment tool that can be used to look at both individual and organisational leadership capability and capacity.

Another useful source of guidance for leaders and senior managers is the Foundation for Good Governance's *Ten Essential Ingredients for Good Governance*. This was developed following some research into non profit organisations but the basic principles are equally relevant to the NHS.

Ten Essential ingredients for Good Governance

- Make sure that the organisation's key documents (constitution, trust deed, strategy and values, statement of compliance, risk assessments) and other such statements are read and understood by the board and staff
- Make sure that all members of the board and staff read and understand the organisation's business or other plans, and that there are clear priorities or targets, budgets and financial information to match the plan
- Ensure the organisation has the right mix of people, skills and abilities to support and develop the organisation and its plan
- Have a written and up-to-date set of policies and procedures (incorporating the relevant codes of conduct and openness) to guide the organisation and ensure everyone is working in a coherent way
- Take meetings seriously. Most of the board's work is carried out in meetings – so how they are run requires regular attention
- Make sure board members are well informed – they cannot fulfil their role without quality information. Well-prepared reports, papers and proposals distributed in advance of meetings play a part in achieving quality decisions

- Ensure that financial reporting is given due importance, and that board members can understand what is being said and recommended. Do not rely on decisions made 'on advice' or 'in good faith'. That is a high-risk strategy
- Spend time on building good relationships, including with partner organisations – these underpin and determine the quality of discussion and decision making
- Ensure the board understands its responsibility to manage the most senior managers, and that it has the capacity and capability to do this
- The board should provide the direction and leadership the organisation needs.

Key questions for the organisation to consider

1. Does the organisation have a distinctive ethos or culture? If so, is this widely shared among people within the organisation? How do we confirm that this is the case in practice? Is this ethos consistent with the principles of good governance? If the answer to any of these questions is no, what are we doing to address this?
2. Do the board and senior managers lead by example and set the organisation's overall tone? If not how can this be achieved?
3. Does the organisation have a meaningful vision/values statement that is communicated to all staff?
4. Are the Nolan principles widely known, understood and adhered to throughout the organisation? If so, are they applied in practice? How do we know this? If the answer to any of these questions is no, what are we doing to change things?
5. Are the principles and values of the *NHS Constitution* widely known, understood and accepted within the organisation? If so, are they applied in practice? How do we know this? If the answer to any of these questions is no, what are we doing to change things?
6. Are attitudes and behaviour within the organisation in accordance with the NHS codes of conduct, accountability and openness? How do we know that this is the case? What are we doing to address any lack of awareness and compliance?
7. Are all staff made aware of the *Code of Conduct for NHS Managers* and the need for compliance? If not how are we planning to address this?
8. Is the quality of leadership clear and effective throughout the organisation? How do we know? What do we need to do differently if there are problems?

This chapter's main learning points

- An organisation's culture must be in tune with the principles of governance
- Those working in the public sector should adhere to Nolan's seven principles of public life
- All providers and commissioners of NHS care have a statutory duty to have regard to the *NHS Constitution* in all their decisions and actions
- The pledges, principles, values and responsibilities set out in the *NHS Constitution* need to be fully embedded into everything the NHS does
- Board members must follow the *Code of Conduct for NHS Boards*, which emphasises the importance of accountability, probity and openness

- Best practice guidance for foundation trusts is set out in Monitor's *Code of Governance*
- The Department of Health's *Code of Practice on Openness* states that the NHS should respond positively to information requests other than in circumstances set out in the code
- For NHS managers, the Department of Health's *Code of Conduct for NHS Managers* sets out the core standards expected
- Good leadership and management are crucial to good governance.

Further reading

The Good Governance Standard for Public Services, the Independent Commission on Good Governance in Public Services, OPM and CIPFA, 2004:
www.opm.co.uk
www.cipfa.org.uk

Vision and Values: organisational culture and values as a source of competitive advantage, CIPD, 2004:
www.cipd.co.uk

Seven Principles of Public Life – First report of The Committee on Standards in Public Life, May 1995:
www.public-standards.org.uk/OurWork/First_Report.html

Managing Public Money, HM Treasury:
www.hm-treasury.gov.uk/psr_mpm_index.htm

The NHS Plan, Department of Health, 2000: www.dh.gov.uk/en/Publicationsandstatistics/Publications/PublicationsPolicyandGuidance/DH_4002960

Integrated Governance Handbook, Department of Health, 2006:
www.dh.gov.uk/en/Publicationsandstatistics/Publications/PublicationsPolicyAndGuidance/DH_4128739

NHS Foundation Trust Code of Governance, Monitor:
www.monitor-nhsft.gov.uk/home/our-publications/browse-category/guidance-foundation-trusts/mandatory-guidance/code-governance-

The Code of Accountability for NHS Boards, Department of Health, 2004:
www.dh.gov.uk/en/Publicationsandstatistics/Publications/PublicationsPolicyAndGuidance/DH_4093864

Governing the NHS: a Guide for NHS Boards, Department of Health, 2003:
www.dh.gov.uk/en/Publicationsandstatistics/Publications/PublicationsPolicyAndGuidance/DH_4082638

The Code of Practice on Openness in the NHS, Department of Health, 2003:
www.dh.gov.uk/en/Publicationsandstatistics/Publications/PublicationsPolicyAndGuidance/DH_4050490

Information governance toolkit, Department of Health:
www.igt.connectingforhealth.nhs.uk/about.aspx

Code of Conduct for NHS Managers, Department of Health, 2002:
www.dh.gov.uk/en/Publicationsandstatistics/Publications/PublicationsPolicyAndGuidance/DH_
4005410

NHS Institute for Innovation and Improvement and the Leadership Qualities Framework:
www.institute.nhs.uk/building_capability/general/leadership_qualities_framework.html

10 Tips for Developing Good Governance, Foundation for Good Governance:
http://ffgg.org.uk/data/data/tips.html

Chapter 4: The External Regulatory Framework

Introduction

A key influence on the governance arrangements of all organisations is the environment within which they operate and the statutory and regulatory requirements that they are expected to satisfy. Most NHS organisations are tightly constrained and so it is particularly important that they are aware of their operational context. They also need to have processes in place as part of their overall governance arrangements to enable them to monitor, respond and adhere to legislative and regulatory developments.

This chapter looks at the key external influences that have a direct impact, paying particular attention to the Government itself and the various statutory regulatory and inspection agencies.

The public sector context

In the public services generally there are additional pressures resulting both from the political environment and the ever-increasing expectations of the public. A failing in one organisation can raise doubts about others in the same field and – in some cases – about the public sector as a whole. This is particularly marked in the NHS, which has always been high profile in political terms.

The role of government

Given that it is a top political priority, it is no surprise that the Government devotes considerable time and effort to ensuring that the NHS operates in an accountable and open way and that it achieves agreed objectives and targets. It is also important to remember that all NHS bodies are creatures of statute – they must always act within the law and never beyond their legal powers. All their powers come from Parliament, through Acts and statutory instruments.

In constitutional terms, the Secretary of State for Health is responsible for providing a comprehensive health service in England, as set out in Acts of Parliament. The Secretary of State is therefore accountable to Parliament (and ultimately to the electorate) for the functioning of the NHS and its use of resources. The Secretary of State is also responsible for the work of the Department of Health (see below for more detail) and – under the coalition government's planned reforms – will have new duties to promote quality improvement, reduce inequalities and promote research.

The Secretary of State has a direct influence on the governance arrangements of NHS bodies and on their powers and activities – the only exception at present (2011/12) is that NHS foundation trusts (FTs) are regulated by Monitor via a board of governors rather than directly by the Secretary of State.[1]

---

[1] See chapter 9 for more on foundation trusts and the role of Monitor.

The most obvious area where the Secretary of State has an impact is in relation to the overall structure of the health service, which is about to undergo substantial change with the abolition from April 2013 of strategic health authorities and PCTs and the introduction of a new NHS Commissioning Board and clinical commissioning groups (see later in this chapter for more).

At a more detailed level, the Secretary of State sets down the statutory powers, structures and reporting lines for different types of organisation. Requirements and duties that NHS organisations must follow are set out in primary and secondary legislation and in circulars, directions and guidelines – these are issued via the Department of Health (see below).

One of the key accountability mechanisms for Parliament is the Health Select Committee – a cross-party committee that is appointed, on behalf of the House of Commons, to examine the 'expenditure, administration and policy of the Department of Health (and any associated public bodies)'.[2]

Two other Parliamentary committees scrutinise the health service:

- the Public Accounts Committee (PAC), which keeps a check on all public expenditure including money spent on health and examines value for money reports from the National Audit Office. The PAC has also issued influential reports on aspects of governance (see chapter 1)
- the Public Administration Select Committee, which examines the reports of the Parliamentary and Health Service Ombudsmen and considers matters relating to the quality and standards of civil service administration.

Parliamentary accountability and scrutiny also means that managers in the NHS must provide information when requested to ministers so that MPs' questions can be answered.

The role of the Department of Health

The Department of Health is accountable to Parliament and the public and its overall aim is 'to improve the health and well-being of the people of England'. The *Statement of NHS Accountability* states that to achieve this aim, the Department:

- 'develops the strategy and direction for the healthcare system
- develops the legislative framework
- secures and allocates resources for healthcare services.'

The Department of Health is also responsible for setting the strategic framework for adult social care and currently takes the lead on public health matters such as environmental hazards, infectious diseases, health promotion and education, safety of medicines and ethical issues.

---

[2] House of Commons Standing Order no 152.

The Department is also responsible for allocating funding to PCTs, managing performance against its statutory responsibilities and (at a more detailed level) issuing guidelines to assist in the implementation of policy objectives. The most accessible and comprehensive source of guidance is the weekly chief executive's bulletin – 'The Week'. This bulletin alerts chief executives to publications, circulars and announcements issued by the Department. There are also monthly and quarterly bulletins titled 'The Month' and 'The Quarter'.

Although its overarching objective will remain the same, the changes planned by the coalition government will see the Department allocating resources received from the Treasury not to PCTs (which will cease to exist from 2013) but to a new independent NHS Commissioning Board that will then decide on funding levels for new clinical commissioning groups and commission some services itself. The Department's role in relation to public health will also change with the introduction of a new public health service – Public Health England. Although Public Health England will be established within the Department, it will work closely with local authorities who will take on primary responsibility at local level for health improvement and reducing health inequalities.

The role of strategic health authorities

To help the Department of Health achieve its aims strategic health authorities (SHAs) have been set up across England to act as NHS regional headquarters. SHAs are 'accountable for the performance and management of the healthcare system'.[3] At present they are responsible for:

- ensuring that patients have access to high quality services
- overseeing the performance of NHS trusts and PCTs
- supporting NHS trusts to reach foundation trust status
- strategic leadership
- organisational and workforce development.

SHAs are directly accountable to the Department of Health. They do not have a role in relation to foundation trusts.

Until October 2011, there were 10 regionally based SHAs but these have now been grouped into 4 clusters, each with a single shared board. In 2013, SHAs will be abolished.

The role of arm's length bodies

Arm's length bodies (ALBs) are stand alone national organisations sponsored by the Department of Health to undertake functions to facilitate the delivery of its agenda. They range in size but tend to have boards, employ staff and publish accounts. Some ALBs are accountable to the Department while others (executive non-departmental public bodies) are created by primary legislation and are accountable directly to Parliament. Uniquely, the Department has a third class of ALB – special health authorities – that are created by secondary legislation.

---

[3] *Statement of NHS Accountability*, Department of Health, 2009.

At present (2011/12) there are four functional categories of ALB:

- regulatory – these are the ALBs that hold health and social care organisations to account and are usually independent. They include the Care Quality Commission (which is looked at in detail later on in this chapter), the Human Fertilisation and Embryology Authority and the Human Tissue Authority
- standards – ALBs that establish national standards and best practice i.e. the National Institute for Health and Clinical Excellence (NICE)
- public welfare – these ALBs focus primarily on safety and the protection of the public and patients (for example, the National Patient Safety Agency and the Health Protection Agency)
- central services to the NHS – which provide services and expertise across the health and social care system (for example, NHS Business Services Authority, Appointments Commission and NHS Litigation Authority).

A review published by the coalition government soon after it came to power in May 2010 reduces the number of ALBs from 18 to 6 with some abolished (for example, the Appointments Commission and the Alcohol Education and Research Council) and others merged (for example, the Health Protection Agency and the National Treatment Agency for Substance Misuse will become part of the new Public Health Service).

The ALBs that will remain once the process of abolition/merger is completed are:

- Monitor (at present the regulator of NHS foundation trusts)
- The National Institute for Health and Clinical Excellence (NICE)
- Care Quality Commission (CQC)
- Information Centre for Health and Social Care
- Medicines and Healthcare Products Regulatory Agency
- NHS Blood and Transplant.

The shape of the NHS

Before we move on to look at the key regulatory and inspection agencies that operate within the health arena it is helpful to see how NHS organisations themselves link back to Parliament. The diagrams that follow make clear what the relationships are both under the existing (2011/12) regime and after the coalition government's planned reforms are implemented.

Current NHS structure

In this diagram the thin arrows indicate a statutory relationship in accountability terms – for example, PCTs (but not the GPs, dentists, opticians or pharmacists that they commission services from) are directly accountable to SHAs. SHAs are accountable to the Department of Health which is in turn accountable (via the Secretary of State) to Parliament. The thick arrows represent planning, commissioning and agreeing of care. Note that ambulance trusts also work with the 999 system to respond to emergencies – this is regarded as part of primary care.

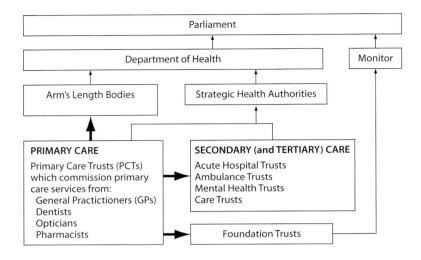

Proposed NHS structure

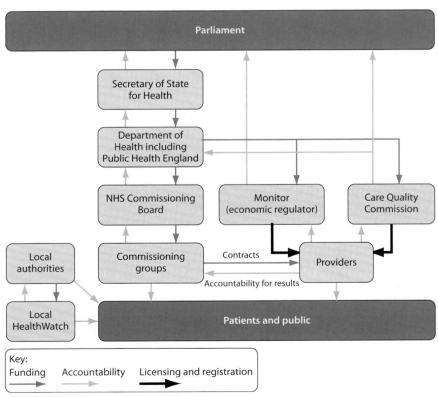

The role of regulatory/inspection and audit agencies

The NHS in England is subject to regulation and inspection from a wide range of bodies that are independent of government and the NHS. These include national agencies and specific organisations linked to the many different professions involved in the delivery of healthcare – ranging from the Royal Colleges to auditors and the Care Quality Commission, the General Medical Council to HM Revenue and Customs.

In an environment where demonstrating high quality performance and the effective use of public funds is essential, the role of regulatory and inspection agencies and their impact on an organisation's reputation and morale cannot be underestimated. It is therefore critical that NHS bodies are aware of the approach and requirements of each organisation and that mechanisms are in place to facilitate the inspection process and respond to any recommendations or advice that is issued.

Audit Commission

The Audit Commission is a non-departmental public body sponsored by the Department for Communities and Local Government. It is responsible for ensuring that public money is spent economically, efficiently and effectively to achieve high quality public services and better outcomes for everyone. In relation to the NHS it is the Audit Commission that currently is responsible for the financial audit regime of SHAs, PCTs and NHS trusts. NHS foundation trusts select and appoint their own external auditors who are regulated by Monitor in line with its own *Audit Code*.

The Audit Commission's role is to:

- appoint external auditors (from its own audit practice or accountancy firms) who audit each body's annual financial statements
- set the required standards of appointed auditors
- regulate the quality of audits.

External auditors must follow the Audit Commission's *Code of Audit Practice* which requires them to review and report on:

- the annual accounts
- arrangements for securing economy, efficiency and effectiveness in the use of resources.

By exception, auditors must also report when the statement on internal control (SIC) does not comply with Department of Health requirements.

The Audit Commission Act 1998 provides auditors with the power to report where they have specific concerns arising from their audits of NHS organisations via:

- public interest reports – section 8 of the Act requires auditors to consider whether to issue a report in the public interest on any significant matter coming to their notice
- reference to the Secretary of State – section 19 requires the auditor to refer matters to the Secretary of State for Health if he or she has reason to believe that an NHS organisation has made a decision that involves, or may involve, unlawful expenditure.

The external auditor is required to issue an annual audit letter to board members at the conclusion of each year's audit. The letter acts as a brief for the board and summarises the major issues arising from the audit which the auditor wishes to raise.

Soon after it came to power, the coalition government announced that the Audit Commission is to be abolished.

Care Quality Commission

The Care Quality Commission (CQC) was established to regulate the essential standards of quality and safety, which are set out in the *Health and Social Care Act 2008*. The CQC took over the activities of the Commission for Social Care Inspection, the Healthcare Commission and the Mental Health Act Commission on 1 April 2009.

CQC was given a range of legal powers and duties as part of the *Health and Social Care Act 2008*, these include:

- registering providers of healthcare and social care to ensure they are meeting the essential standards of quality and safety
- monitoring how providers comply with the standards by gathering information and visiting them when CQC think it is needed
- using enforcement powers, such as fines and public warnings and closing down services, if services drop below the essential standards and particularly if the CQC think that people's rights or safety are at risk
- acting to protect patients whose rights are restricted under the *Mental Health Act*
- promoting improvement in services by conducting regular reviews of how well those who arrange and provide services locally are performing
- carrying out special reviews of particular types of services and pathways of care, or investigations on areas where CQC has concerns about quality and safety
- seeking the views of people who use services and involving them in CQC's work
- telling people about the quality of their local care services to help providers and commissioners of services to learn from each other about what works best and where improvement is needed, and help to shape national policy.

Registration and compliance system

CQC regulates through a registration and compliance system, where registration represents a licence to operate. Once registered to carry on regulated activities a provider must show that it is meeting the essential standards of quality and safety.

CQC monitors a provider's compliance with essential standards using a system of information management and analysis, which informs inspection visits to registered services. CQC uses and checks many different types of information about providers, including clinical performance data and information from people who use services, public representative groups, and other organisations and regulators, such as Monitor.

NHS providers have been registered with CQC since1 April 2010. Adult social care and independent healthcare providers were registered between April and October 2010. Dentists and private ambulances have been registered from April 2011 onwards. NHS out-of-hours services that are not GP practices will be registered by 1 April 2012. NHS walk-in centres that do not provide out of hours services and GPs will be registered by April 2013.

Essential standards of quality and safety

As mentioned above, the essential standards are set out in the *Health and Social Care Act 2008 (Regulated Activities) Regulations 2010*, and the *Care Quality Commission (Registration) Regulations 2009*. These regulations describe 28 essential standards of quality and safety that people who use health and adult social care services should expect.

CQC looks at all 28 essential standards when monitoring the compliance of providers, but its judgement framework has a particular focus on the 16 essential standards and associated outcomes that most directly relate to the quality and safety of care experienced by people using a service. The 16 essential standards are:

- care and welfare of people who use services
- assessing and monitoring the quality of service provision
- safeguarding vulnerable people who use services
- cleanliness and infection control
- management of medicines
- meeting nutritional needs
- safety and suitability of premises
- safety, availability and suitability of equipment
- respecting and involving people who use services
- consent to care and treatment
- complaints management
- records management
- requirements relating to workers
- staffing
- supporting workers
- cooperating with other providers.

Conditions of registration

When providers first register with CQC they might have compliance conditions attached to their registration where CQC has identified concerns about non-compliance. Providers must implement an agreed time-bound improvement plan for the conditions to be removed or CQC will take enforcement action.

In addition, CQC can apply 'routine restrictive conditions' to providers as part of their registration. These conditions will place a limit or a restriction on what activity can be carried out. It may be linked to a location, regulated activity, service type, or specific activity. An example of a routine restrictive condition is defining a location where a regulated activity can be carried out or the need for a registered manager. If changes occur to a service that impact on the routine restrictive conditions, the provider must inform CQC and apply for a variation to their registration or face enforcement action.

CQC in the future

Under the *Health and Social Care Bill* the CQC will continue to regulate through a registration and compliance system, but the Bill will result in several changes for CQC, in particular:

- the creation of HealthWatch England within CQC, which will also involve working with the Local HealthWatch entities that are to replace Local Involvement Networks (LINks)
- the introduction of a joint licensing regime for NHS providers with Monitor
- the integration of certain functions of the Human Fertilisation and Embryology Authority, Human Tissue Authority, and National Information Governance Board for Health and Social Care into CQC.

Further information on CQC's regulatory activities can be found on its website at: www.cqc.org.uk

Monitor

Monitor is an independent corporate body established under the *Health and Social Care (Community Health and Standards) Act 2003*. At present it is responsible for 'authorising, monitoring and regulating NHS foundation trusts'[4] and is directly accountable to Parliament.

Under the new NHS structure, Monitor will continue to oversee FTs until 2016 but will expand into a wider economic regulator for the health and social care sectors with an overarching duty to protect and promote patients' interests. Monitor will be responsible for licensing all providers of NHS-funded care in England, including existing foundation trusts, private and voluntary sector providers. In carrying out its licensing role, Monitor will be required to co-operate with the CQC which will continue to be responsible for registering providers against 'essential levels of safety and quality'. Monitor and the CQC are to establish a single integrated process of licensing and registration.

Monitor will also work with the new NHS Commissioning Board to:

- ensure continuity of services (i.e. where services at risk of closure are essential and there is no viable alternative)
- set and regulate prices for NHS funded services with Monitor focusing on designing the pricing methodology and using it to set prices and the Commissioning Board developing the pricing structure.

In terms of its own funding, Monitor will levy fees on those it registers to support the cost of its licensing-related activities with its other regulatory activities being funded by the Treasury.

Chapter 9 of this guide looks in detail at foundation trust governance but the key point to note at this stage is that foundation trusts currently operate under a different regulatory and financial regime to the rest of the NHS.

---

[4] www.monitor-nhsft.gov.uk

National Audit Office (NAO)

The National Audit Office (NAO) reports to Parliament on the spending of central government money. To be able to do this the NAO:

- conducts financial audits of all Government departments and agencies and many other public bodies – this includes the Department of Health
- reports to Parliament on the value for money with which public bodies have spent public money.

As well as producing their own resource accounts the Department is required to produce summarised accounts for SHAs, NHS trusts, PCTs and each of the ALBs whilst Monitor produces consolidated accounts for FTs. When auditing the Department's and Monitor's accounts, the NAO places reliance on and takes assurance from the work carried out by auditors on the underlying accounts of individual NHS bodies. In addition, the results of NAO reports affect the Department and these can in turn have an impact at local level.

Local authorities

Since January 2003, local authorities with social services responsibilities have been able to establish committees of councillors to provide overview and scrutiny of local NHS bodies by virtue of powers set out in section 38 of the *Local Government Act 2000*. The ultimate aim is to secure health improvement for local communities by encouraging authorities to look beyond their own service responsibilities to issues of wider concern to local people. This is achieved by giving democratically elected representatives the right to scrutinise how local health services are provided and developed for their constituents.

Once the coalition government's planned changes are implemented, local authorities will have a stronger role in supporting patient choice, ensuring local involvement and leading on health improvement and reducing health inequalities. In particular, they will lead the joint strategic needs assessment (at present this a joint responsibility with PCTs), via newly established health and wellbeing boards which will have a duty to involve users and the public. These health and wellbeing boards will also work with the new clinical commissioning groups to ensure that commissioning plans meet local needs. This approach is designed to provide strategic co-ordination to the commissioning of NHS services, social care and health improvement. Members of clinical commissioning groups will be represented on the health and wellbeing boards. Local authorities will jointly commission some services with commissioning groups and appoint a Director of Public Health in conjunction with the newly established public health service – Public Health England.

Other external bodies

There is a wide range of other organisations with an interest in health which can affect governance arrangements. These include:

- professional bodies on both the clinical and managerial side. These organisations often have their own codes of conduct and disciplinary regimes that apply to their members. For example, the Royal Colleges and other independent audit and assurance bodies that provide an assurance to NHS organisations

- other government departments and agencies – for example, the Cabinet Office and Department for Communities and Local Government
- non departmental public bodies, independent and local organisations (for example, local involvement networks – in the future HealthWatch)
- representative bodies – for example, the British Medical Association (BMA), the NHS Confederation and UNISON
- think tanks and research organisations such as the King's Fund
- the public – NHS organisations are required to engage with the public and conduct meaningful consultations.

Key questions for the organisation to consider

1. Do we understand how our organisation fits into the NHS structure – both now and in the future?
2. How do we ensure that we are aware of and meet our statutory and regulatory requirements?
3. Do we understand the role of the Secretary of State and Department of Health in relation to our organisation?
4. (For FTs) do we understand the role of Monitor in relation to our organisation?
5. (For NHS trusts and PCTs at present) do we understand the role of the Strategic Health Authority in relation to our organisation?
6. Do we understand the role of the Care Quality Commission in relation to our organisation?
7. Do we understand the role of the external auditors in relation to our organisation?
8. Are we well informed and updated on the reports issued by these bodies? Do we look out for learning points and act upon them?
9. Does our organisation respond appropriately to the requirements of these bodies?
10. Do we respond to and learn from the external auditor's reports on our organisation?
11. Do we establish constructive relationships with all these external organisations and do we ensure that they understand our objectives and approach?

This chapter's main learning points

- The external environment is a major influence on NHS bodies – political pressures and public expectations are particularly marked
- All NHS organisations need to monitor, respond and adhere to legislative and regulatory developments and ensure that their governance arrangements make this possible
- All powers that NHS bodies have come from Parliament
- The Secretary of State is accountable to Parliament for the functioning of the NHS and the use of resources
- Monitor is responsible to Parliament for NHS foundation trusts
- Regulatory and inspection agencies help ensure that NHS organisations are functioning as they should

- Key regulators/ inspection agencies in the healthcare arena are Monitor, the Audit Commission, the Care Quality Commission and the National Audit Office
- There is a wide range of other organisations that can affect governance arrangements including professional bodies, local authorities, other government departments and research organisations.

Further reading

Statement of NHS Accountability, Department of Health, 2010:
www.dh.gov.uk/en/Publicationsandstatistics/Publications/PublicationsPolicyAndGuidance/DH_093422

The Week, Chief Executive's Bulletin, Department of Health: www.dh.gov.uk/en/Publicationsandstatistics/Bulletins/theweek/index.htm

Monitor: www.monitor-nhsft.gov.uk

Strategic Health Authorities: www.nhs.uk/NHSEngland/aboutnhs/Pages/Authoritiesandtrusts.aspx#q07

Arm's Length Bodies: www.dh.gov.uk/en/Aboutus/OrganisationsthatworkwithDH/Armslengthbodies/DH_063363

The Audit Commission (including details of public interest reports): www.audit-commission.gov.uk

Health and Social Care Act 2008:
www.dh.gov.uk/en/Publicationsandstatistics/Legislation/Actsandbills/HealthandSocialCareBill/index.htm

Care Quality Commission:
www.cqc.org.uk

The National Audit Office:
www.nao.org.uk

Chapter 5: Organisational Structures: Running an NHS Organisation

Introduction

A key part of any governance framework is that there must be absolute clarity about who is responsible for what. For most NHS bodies, it is the Government (via the Secretary of State and the Department of Health) that sets down the structural arrangements that must be followed for the 'top' management and leadership structures. The only exception is foundation trusts (FTs) where structures are set down by Monitor, the independent regulator.

This chapter focuses on how NHS organisations are structured under the current regime (2011/12) and who is responsible for what. Although structures vary according to the type of organisation, two basic principles apply to all – each must have its own board and an 'accountable (or accounting in FTs) officer'. Once the coalition government's planned changes are introduced this will remain the case with the new clinical commissioning groups required to have in place as a minimum a:

- 'governing group' (with decision making powers, at least two lay members, at least one registered nurse and a doctor who is a secondary care specialist)[1]
- chief executive officer who is the accountable officer
- chief finance officer.

They will also need to have a defined management structure that is able to demonstrate that they are using public money as they should and operating in a transparent and accountable way. However, the coalition government has not specified in detail what the management structure should look like.

Where does the power lie?
The role of governors, boards, committees and executive directors

Governors

Unlike other NHS organisations, the foundation trust structure includes governors to represent local interests and to 'bind a trust to its patients, service users and stakeholders'.[2] These governors consist of both elected and appointed individuals who represent FT members and other stakeholder organisations through a board of governors. Governors do not get involved with the FT's day to day running – instead their key role is to challenge the trust's board of directors and hold them to account for the trust's performance. For more about the role of governors in FTs, see chapter 9.

---

[1] *Government response to NHS Future Forum report,* 14 June 2011.
[2] *Your Statutory Duties: a Reference Guide for NHS Foundation Trust Governors,* Monitor, 2009.

The board

Purpose

At present (2011/12), each NHS organisation operates with a pre-eminent governing body that takes corporate responsibility for the strategies and actions of the organisation and is accountable to the public and parliament. This governing body or board sets the strategy and objectives for the organisation, monitors their achievement, and looks for potential problems and risks that might prevent them achieving those objectives. The board also expects to receive assurances that things are working as they should.

This overall responsibility is set out in the National Leadership Council's report *The Healthy NHS Board: principles for good governance* which was issued following the failings and subsequent reviews of Mid-Staffordshire NHS Foundation Trust. It says that 'the purpose of NHS boards is to govern effectively and in doing so to build public and stakeholder confidence that their health and healthcare is in safe hands'.

Composition

The board brings together in a decision-making forum the executive directors and the non-executive directors (NEDs) of the organisation and is separate from the day-to-day management structure. Generally the boards of non foundation NHS trusts that are not teaching hospitals and strategic health authorities (SHAs) comprise a chair, five executives (including the chief executive and the director of finance) and five non-executives. In primary care trusts (PCTs) the executive board members must also include the professional executive committee (PEC) chair, a GP and a nurse. Each board is led by an independent, non-executive chair.

The coalition government has stated that under the new regime (after PCTs and SHAs cease to exist) each clinical commissioning group's governing body will have independent membership via at least two lay members (equivalent to NEDs), one registered nurse and one doctor who is a secondary care specialist. The two lay members will be key appointments with specific responsibilities: one will have a lead role in patient and public involvement, while the other will oversee key elements of the governance arrangements including audit. In addition, one of the lay members will undertake the role of the group's chair or the deputy chair.

NEDs play a particularly important role on the board by providing independence, constructive challenge and a breadth of experience. By balancing the views of the executive directors, NEDs ensure that power is not concentrated in a few hands such that no individual or small group of individuals can dominate the board's decision making.

Constructive challenge in boards – good practice tip

Constructive challenge is the key to good accountability and should be the watchword for **all** board members. Its focus is on accentuating the positive, asking questions that probe into a little more detail, not in the hope of catching someone out, but with the intention of gaining knowledge.

A good officer welcomes this approach, as it enables them to test the management arrangements that they have in place and, if gaps are found, provides an opportunity to improve. This applies equally to all board members (executive and non-executive), who must be prepared to challenge to increase their level of understanding and assurance.

Reactions to challenge also help to build up trust and credibility. A confident (but not over-confident) response to a question by a director will engender trust and assurance that he/she knows their area of management – the converse also being true.

At the other extreme, 'destructive' challenge can lead to a more defensive and insular relationship, potentially resulting in key issues being avoided or hidden. It is a fine balance, but one that boards need to keep under review.

The chair has an important role to play in this area leading by example and encouraging an open and constructive approach.

At present, the NHS Appointments Commission is responsible for appointing, re-appointing (and where necessary terminating) chairs and NEDs to the boards of SHAs, PCTs and NHS trusts. Appointees are chosen from lay people within the community that the organisation serves and are selected with a view to ensuring a balance of skills and experience. For example, there may be NEDs with professional qualifications in law or accountancy and others who have experience as a user of NHS services. Once the coalition government's planned changes are introduced (with both SHAs and PCTs ceasing to exist), any appointments will be made by the Department of Health.

FTs are responsible for appointing their own directors and Monitor's *Code of Governance* recommends that there 'should be a formal, rigorous and transparent procedure for the appointment or election of new members to the boards of directors' and that appointments should be made 'on merit and based on objective criteria.' To ensure that this is the case in practice, the Code recommends a nomination committee (or two separate nomination committees) for executive and non executive appointments to ensure that independence is enshrined in the process and appointments are made on the basis of need (in terms of the board's needs) and competency (in relation to the individual's ability). Monitor's guidance states that it is 'desirable' for there to be a majority of governor votes on nominations committees.

Monitor's *Code of Governance* also recommends that the board of directors appoint a 'senior independent director' from amongst the NEDs (in consultation with the board of governors) so that there is someone to deal with concerns of governors and/or members that cannot be resolved through 'normal channels' (i.e. via the chair, the chief executive, or finance director). See chapter 9 for more about FT governance arrangements.

Accountability

At present, chairs and NEDs of SHAs, PCTs and NHS trusts are accountable to the Secretary of State and are expected to:

- hold the executive to account
- use their skills and experience to help the board as it develops health strategies
- ensure the delivery of high quality services to patients
- make sure that the interests of patients remain paramount.

In addition, wider public accountability is achieved via consultation exercises, public meetings and published annual reports.

Roles and responsibilities

A board's prime duty is to 'add value to the organisation, enabling it to deliver healthcare and health improvement within the law and without causing harm. It does this by providing a framework within which the organisation can thrive and grow'.

In line with the criteria set out in the Higgs report on the role and effectiveness of NEDs (see chapter 1), the board is responsible for:

- observing collective responsibility for adding value to the organisation – promoting the organisation's success and directing and supervising its affairs
- leadership within a framework of prudent and effective control which enables risk to be assessed and managed
- looking ahead – setting the strategic aims, ensuring resources are sufficient and managing performance
- setting and maintaining values.

As the board is the pre-eminent governing body, there is a range of responsibilities and decisions that it cannot delegate. These are sometimes referred to as being 'reserved' to the board and include:

- financial stewardship responsibilities (for example, adopting the annual report and accounts)
- determining the organisation's strategy and policies and setting its strategic direction
- appointing senior executives
- overseeing the delivery of services
- standards of governance and behaviour.

The board is free to agree other issues that only it will deal with and must also decide which responsibilities it will delegate. To help the board discharge its role effectively there are a number of other committees – some of them mandatory – that need to exist. These are discussed briefly below.

For more detail on the role of the chair/NEDs see the NHS Appointments Commission 2003 guide – *Governing the NHS: a Guide for NHS Boards*.

Liability

NEDs of NHS bodies are normally considered to be personally liable for their actions and decisions either taken personally or as a board member. The risk of legal action arising from this liability is very small but NHS bodies may issue an indemnity for the reassurance of members. In 1999 the Committee on Standards in Public Life recommended the following wording for such indemnity: 'A chairman or non-executive member or director who has acted honestly and in good faith will not have to meet out of his or her own personal resources any personal civil liability which is incurred in the execution or purported execution of his or her board function, save where the person has acted recklessly'.

Board behaviour – good practice tip

A consistent lesson from governance failings, as well as external reviews, is that the majority of organisations that have encountered problems had the appropriate arrangements in place (for example, Enron had an audit committee), but these arrangements were not 'effective' (Enron's audit committee members were not probing hard enough at the issues which, possibly with the advantage of hindsight, they should have been). Often the key is the behaviour of board members – some 'top tips' are:

- there should be regular reviews of the number/structure of committees that report to the board to make sure they have meaningful roles in the organisation and are effective
- deal with the detail outside the board room. Spelling and grammar errors, or small calculation mistakes do happen, but board time is precious and should be used well
- executive directors should welcome constructive challenge – it is one of those things that is 'good for you'
- build in regular self evaluation of performance of the board to ask the leading question: 'are we performing as well as we may?' This should be carried out in the spirit of continuous improvement, rather than self-congratulation
- the role of the chair and chief executive in providing leadership to the board should be debated openly
- an open culture which allows challenge within the context of collective responsibility should be promoted
- the assurance framework[3] should be a key driver behind the board's agenda.

Audit committee

At present, every NHS organisation (including FTs) must have an audit committee that reports to the board. This is made clear in the HFMA's *NHS Audit Committee Handbook*, which states that: 'NHS board members have a daunting task in overseeing some of the largest and most complex organisations in the country. To fulfil this role it is the board's responsibility to put in place governance structures and processes to:

- ensure that the organisation operates effectively and meets its strategic objectives
- provide the board with assurance that this is the case.

---

[3] Assurance frameworks are looked at in detail in chapter 7.

However, even the best structures and processes can let down an organisation if they and the assurances they provide are not operated with sufficient rigour. Boards can, and should, look to their audit committee to review and report on the relevance and rigour of the governance structures in place and the assurances the board receives'.

The distinctive characteristic of the audit committee is that it comprises only non-executive directors – there must be at least three, with a quorum of two. The fact that only NEDs can be members allows the committee to operate independently of any executive management processes and to apply an objective approach in the conduct of its business.

The chair of the organisation should not be a member of the audit committee and will not normally attend. The chief executive and all other executive directors will attend whenever they are invited by the committee chair and, in particular, to provide assurances and explanations to the committee when it is discussing audit reports or other matters within their areas of responsibility.

The *Audit Committee Handbook* contains a wealth of information about the role of audit committees, their key functions and how they should be organised. In particular it recognises that: 'the requirement for a Statement on Internal Control, informed by an embedded system of assurance, and clear evidence of fitness to register with the Care Quality Commission, mean that boards and audit committees must consider the whole system of internal control. To carry this out effectively:

- boards and their audit committees need to review their respective terms of reference and scheme of delegation to ensure that their roles and authority are distinct, appropriate and effective
- audit committees must have a broad remit, encompassing clinical, financial and all operational risks in order that they are able to take a comprehensive view of governance, risk management and internal control across the organisation
- both boards and audit committees must recognise the pivotal role their assurance framework should play in managing the organisation's strategic objectives
- audit committees need to look at the ways that they work and consider how they can be more effective
- while broadening their remit, audit committees should continue to maintain a focus on achieving strong financial management across the organisation that will underpin operational developments
- in the context of likely future funding constraints, audit committees need to maintain a systematic approach that considers and measures the potential impact of proposed cost reductions on the quality of healthcare.'

The specimen terms of reference in the *Handbook* further emphasise the audit committee's role in relation to governance by making clear that one of its key duties is to 'review the establishment and maintenance of an effective system of integrated governance, risk management and internal control, across the whole of the organisation's activities (both clinical and non-clinical), that supports the achievement of the organisation's objectives.

In particular, the committee will review the adequacy and effectiveness of:

- all risk and control related disclosure statements (in particular the Statement on Internal Control/annual governance statement), together with any accompanying head of internal audit statement, external audit opinion or other appropriate independent assurances, prior to endorsement by the board
- the underlying assurance processes that indicate the degree of achievement of corporate objectives, the effectiveness of the management of principal risks and the appropriateness of the above disclosure statements
- the policies for ensuring compliance with relevant regulatory, legal and code of conduct requirements and related reporting and self-certification
- the policies and procedures for all work related to fraud and corruption as set out in Secretary of State Directions and as required by NHS Protect.

In carrying out this work the committee will primarily utilise the work of internal audit, external audit and other assurance functions, but will not be limited to these sources. It will also seek reports and assurances from directors and managers as appropriate, concentrating on the over-arching systems of integrated governance, risk management and internal control, together with indicators of their effectiveness. This will be evidenced through the committee's use of an effective assurance framework to guide its work and that of the audit and assurance functions that report to it.'

It is important to note that the audit committee is not responsible for establishing and maintaining processes for governance – that is a role that executive directors and the accountable/accounting officer (the chief executive) must fulfil. The audit committee's focus is on scrutinising the way in which these processes operate. Equally, an organisation's line managers have the prime responsibility for managing risk, which they do by applying controls to mitigate it. The audit committee's role in this area is to:

- obtain assurance that controls work as intended
- challenge poor sources of assurance.

The coalition government's plans do not yet include a requirement for clinical commissioning groups to have an audit committee. However, as mentioned earlier, one of the lay members on the governing group will be required to play a lead role in relation to 'key elements of governance such as audit, remuneration and managing conflicts of interest'.

Remuneration committee

The remuneration (and terms of service) committee is another committee that is currently mandatory for all NHS organisations (including FTs) and reports to the board. Its role is to advise the board about the pay, other benefits and terms of employment for the chief executive and other senior staff. To ensure that people involved in the day-to-day running of the organisation do not make sensitive decisions, the committee's membership comprises the organisation's chair and at least two other NEDs. The chief executive may attend other than when his or her own position is being considered.

In FTs, the recommendation in Monitor's *Code of Governance* is that the remuneration committee should be composed of NEDs including at least three who are independent. In this context, an independent NED is one who is determined by the board of directors to be 'independent in character and judgement' with no relationships or circumstances that 'are likely to affect, or could appear to affect, the director's judgement' (see Code provision A.3.1).

The coalition government's plans do not yet include a requirement for clinical commissioning groups to have a remuneration committee. However, as mentioned earlier, one of the lay members on the governing group will be required to play a lead role in this area.

Professional executive committee

At present (and until they cease to exist in 2013), all PCTs must have a professional executive committee (PEC). The PEC is a committee of the PCT's board and is designed to bring together clinical and managerial perspectives. It is important that the PEC's responsibilities are clearly set out at local level and understood by all board and PEC members. The precise role and structure of PECs varies across PCTs but there are a number of core principles that are common to all. These were set out in guidance issued by the Department of Health in 2007:

- PECs need to be patient-focussed and promote the health and well-being of communities, as well as addressing health inequalities
- PECs need to be drivers of strong clinical leadership and enablers of clinical empowerment
- PECs need to be decision-making and firmly part of the governance and accountability framework of the PCT
- PECs should reflect a range of clinical professions and the wealth of experience this brings
- PCTs have the freedom to determine how PECs operate according to local circumstances.

This guidance also identified key PEC functions as being:

- supporting the PCT in developing its vision and strategic direction
- commissioning and supporting practice based commissioning
- clinical effectiveness and clinical governance
- leading clinical communications with partners and stakeholders.

The make-up of a PEC is determined locally but must be sufficient to fulfil the functions set out above and should:

- include PCT board director(s)
- have a majority of professionals who should be practising clinicians
- include co-options of staff, clinicians and others (for example, local authority and voluntary organisation representatives, patients and secondary care clinicians) where such skills are needed.

In addition, the PEC chair should be a member of the PCT board.

Other board committees – good practice tip

Boards may establish other committees for specific purposes but it is worth assessing whether:

- each committee has clear terms of reference, related to the board's role and objectives so that its role is a) unambiguous and b) makes a relevant contribution
- it functions effectively (i.e. meets with appropriate frequency, is well attended with minutes that reflect clearly its terms of reference)
- decisions are made, actions are clear and recommendations are followed through at subsequent meetings.

The following calculation may also be useful:

- list all the committees and working groups that report to the board
- identify all those who attend or are involved in some way
- work out, on average, how long each person takes in relation to the meeting, and multiply the number of attendees by the number of hours
- work out the number of times a year that the committee or group meets, and then work out the total number of hours per annum spent on that committee or group
- add up the total number of hours (or days) spent on committees
- assess whether this is effective use of time.

In reviewing its committees the board can use the opportunity to look at its own role, ensuring that there is no overlap and that it is clear about what activities/decisions it has reserved for itself.

Charitable funds committee

Some NHS organisations have charitable funds that are completely separate from NHS monies. These charitable funds are governed not by NHS law but by charity law and the Charity Commission's regulatory regime.

Where such funds exist they are usually managed by a dedicated charitable funds committee that is **not** a committee of the NHS organisation's board. In most cases the funds are managed by 'NHS corporate trustees' – in other words, it is the NHS corporate body (i.e. NHS trusts or special health authorities) that is the trustee. The board of the trust or authority acts on behalf of the corporate trustee in the administration of the charitable funds but the board members are not themselves individual trustees. In practice this means that the charitable funds committee is a committee of board directors, but not a sub-committee of the organisation's board.

Other trustee models do exist in the NHS:

- **special trustees**: under section 7 of the 1946 NHS Act the endowment and trust funds were vested in the board of governors of designated teaching hospitals who acted as trustees. Special trustees are no longer created

- **section 11 trustees:** under s11 (1–3) of the *NHS and Community Care Act 1990* (Re-enacted under paragraph 10, Schedule 4 to the *NHS Act 2006*), the Secretary of State for Health can appoint trustees to hold and administer the charitable funds associated with an NHS trust. Equivalent provision was made (in section 7 of the *Health Act 1999*) for trustees for a primary care trust
- **section 51 trustees:** under s51 of the *NHS Act 2006*, the Secretary of State for Health can appoint trustees to hold and administer the charitable funds associated with an NHS foundation trust.

Detailed guidance about charitable funds is set out in the HFMA's publication *NHS Charitable Funds: a Practical Guide.*

Chief executive/accountable officer

The Department of Health has formally given chief executives the status of 'accountable (or accounting in FTs) officer'. This means that chief executives are accountable to:

- the organisation's board for meeting the objectives it sets, for day-to-day management and for ensuring that governance arrangements are effective
- the Department for the proper stewardship of public money and assets and for the organisation's performance.

The duties of accountable officers are set out in detail in a memorandum issued by the Department of Health's accountable officer and signed by the organisation's chief executive. The key duties are to make sure that their organisations:

- operate effectively, economically and with probity
- use their resources prudently and economically, avoiding waste and extravagance
- keep proper accounts.

The role of the accountable officer is a key element in governance terms with a line of accountability stretching to Parliament as shown below:

Accountability line – 2011/12

Parliament

↑

Secretary of State for Health

↑

Department of Health accountable officer – NHS chief executive and permanent secretary

↑

NHS body accountable officer – chief executive

In FTs the line of accountability is different as accounting officers are responsible to Parliament via Monitor. Monitor has issued its own accounting officer memorandum which emphasises that 'accounting officers are responsible to Parliament for the resources under their control.' The memorandum also states that the accounting officer 'has responsibility for the overall organisation, management and staffing of the NHS FT and for its procedures in financial and other matters'. In particular he or she 'must ensure that:

- there is a high standard of financial management in the NHS FT as a whole
- financial systems and procedures promote the efficient and economical conduct of business and safeguard financial propriety and regularity throughout the whole NHS FT
- financial considerations are fully taken into account in decisions on NHS FT proposals.'

Clearly the relationship between the chief executive and the board is an important one as he or she is responsible for 'ensuring that the board is empowered to govern the organisation and that the objectives it sets are accomplished through effective and properly controlled executive action'.

Under the coalition government's planned changes, both the NHS Commissioning Board (NHSCB) and each clinical commissioning group will have an accountable officer. The accountable officer in each commissioning group will be accountable both to the NHSCB and to the commissioning group.

Each commissioning group will select its accountable officer itself but he or she will be appointed formally by the NHSCB at the time of authorisation. As with other NHS organisations, accountable officers' responsibilities are likely to be set out in a memorandum by the Department and include the requirement to appear before the Public Accounts Committee to give evidence of their and their organisation's performance as requested. The line of accountability will therefore look like this:

> **Line of accountability – from 2013**
>
> Parliament
> ↑
> Secretary of State for Health
> ↑
> Department of Health accounting officer
> ↑
> NHS Commissioning Board accountable officer
> ↑
> Clinical commissioning group accountable officer

Directors of finance

At present, directors of finance of health organisations are automatically executive directors with a seat on the board. The Treasury's guide, *Managing Public Money* (a requirement for central government and recommended good practice for other public organisations) states that the finance director should 'have board status equivalent to other board members' and that he or she should be 'a member of the senior leadership team'.

Their three key responsibilities as identified in the Finance Staff Development Board's guide to *The Role of the Finance Director in a Patient-led NHS – a Guide for NHS Boards* are:

- to provide financial governance and assurance
- to provide business and commercial advice to the board
- corporate responsibilities as an executive director of the board.

The HFMA has also issued a *Policy Statement on the Role of the NHS Finance Director* which recognises that the role of the finance director is one of the most challenging in the NHS with responsibilities ranging from statutory duties relating to accountability, governance and probity; 'traditional' treasurer activities; corporate strategic management and day-to-day operational management. The Statement identifies four core areas of activity:

- corporate leadership and management
- stewardship and accountability
- financial management
- professional leadership and management.

If you want to know more about what each of these roles involves the Statement is available as a free download from the HFMA's website.

Under the coalition government's planned changes each clinical commissioning group will have a chief finance officer although he or she may fulfil that role for more than one commissioning group.

Executive management

Each NHS organisation needs to have in place an effective management structure designed to implement the policies agreed by the board. This structure will vary between organisations but should ensure that all areas of responsibility are clearly accountable to a manager and ultimately to an executive director.

FTs are required by statute and their constitutions to have as executive directors at least a medical director and a nursing director. This is in addition to the chief executive and finance director who are automatically executive directors in all NHS bodies.

Integrated governance

Whilst the presence of well defined structures is important, treating governance issues through functional or compartmentalised processes is unlikely to be effective. An integrated approach to governance pulls together the potentially disparate systems, process and behaviours to:

- allow the board to clearly define its own purpose and strategic direction, within the context of the overall goals established for the NHS
- ensure fitness for purpose, by considering the assurance requirements and the information needs of the board and its supporting structures, including committees.

It is important to recognise that a single, prescribed structure is not appropriate for all organisations – instead, organisations need to be 'self aware' and assess their own governance arrangements. There are two useful guides that can help in this area – the *Integrated Governance Handbook* and *Integrated Governance: a guide to risk and joining up the NHS reforms*. Although neither is prescriptive, these guides set out best practice approaches that will help organisations review their processes and structures. They also provide practical pointers for improvement and include self assessment tools including a 'maturity matrix' so that an organisation can review its progress in integrated governance terms (see appendix 3).

One role that the *Integrated Governance Handbook* focuses on is that of a company secretary with main responsibilities to:

- monitor compliance with relevant legislation
- advise the board and governors on key governance issues
- provide support to the board and its committees.

This is seen as a high level post, appointed by the remuneration committee and answerable to the board. Key to the success of this role is the need to balance being part of the executive management team (so that the post holder has a full understanding of the organisation's business) whilst at the same time remaining a neutral observer and advisor to the board or executive team. Many NHS organisations now have a company secretary role (often called the trust secretary), although the job content may include some responsibility for other areas – for example, risk management, performance management or corporate affairs and communications.

Governance between organisations

Governance structures can come under particular strain when organisations work closely together. Indeed, ineffective partnership working, whether between the NHS and the private sector, or other parts of the public sector is often cited as an issue when governance failings emerge. Given that there is likely to be increased use of the voluntary sector and social enterprise organisations over the coming years, the pressure on structures will be even greater.

The main way of resolving difficulties associated with partnership working is ensuring that there is clarity and understanding, as much through a meeting of minds as in the detailed contractual paperwork. Both sides need to understand each other's objectives, constraints and imperatives, to ensure that the duty of partnership is made to work. These respective expectations and responsibilities should be written down clearly to ensure successful achievement and to avoid any subsequent misunderstandings. Partners should also be clear about the risks that they each retain.

Another way of working that can put pressure on governance structures is sharing or outsourcing services. Where this takes place, the key governance issue is the management of the contract. In particular an NHS organisation must ensure that:

- it is receiving the goods or services that it has outsourced
- there is clarity about its own responsibilities, in terms of information provided, timescales and expectations.

It goes without saying that for all shared services there needs to be good contract management. However, it is important to bear in mind that in governance terms a shared service denotes that the NHS organisation has a stake in the success of the organisation and so should be involved actively in its management and governance. Difficulties can arise when these two elements are either confused, or one of them is omitted altogether – thus undermining the whole concept of 'sharing'.

Mergers and re-organisations

Governance structures and cultures are also challenged whenever organisations merge or re-organise. The key governance issues arising from mergers/re-organisations are:

- how do you keep continuity of the main business, including maintenance of high standards of governance and risk management, whilst managers and staff are naturally anxious about their future? The main answer is through clear communication, but also through clarity of planning and making key decisions as early as possible[4]
- how do you maintain financial control at a time of change, most critically when a board of directors has either not been appointed or not had time to develop organisationally? Experience of mergers indicates that it is always more difficult to recover financial control once it has slipped, than to implement it in the first place
- a part-year merger will always have an impact on the results of a financial cycle that is normally focussed on a 31 March year-end, unless clear continuity is maintained.

Maintaining financial focus – good practice tip

All NHS organisations (other than FTs) have a statutory duty to break-even, but all too often this clashes with the myriad demands of targets and competing resources, especially when there is also restructuring going on. Lessons from governance failures, especially those with a clear financial impact, often involve a failure to monitor finances as a key issue in the escalation of the problem.

What can boards do, to maintain the appropriate financial focus?

- ensure that all members of the board have a basic level of financial literacy. If they have not got this, or cannot achieve it in a rapid timescale, then the board should be reviewing its overall composition very closely. Financial expertise should not be left to one or two specialists, because all actions will have a financial impact
- do not leave finance to the professionals – this is critical. Whilst the chief executive, as accountable officer, and the director of finance have the detailed knowledge, all executive directors are responsible for the commitment of expenditure and, in providers, for the activity that generates income. It is equally important that finance specialists – including the finance director – recognise that their role is not limited to financial issues and that they should be involved in all issues discussed at board level

---

[4] See the HFMA's guide: *Hitting the Fast Lane: Driving Long-term Integration in NHS Mergers*, 2006.

- agree the format of financial reports to the board, with a clear explanation of how to drill down. These reports need to strike a balance between an overview and the supporting detail
- get an assurance that the basic financial information being used by the board to monitor performance and inform decision-making is complete, accurate and valid. Poor internal financial controls can mean that financial information is not worth the paper it is printed on.

The importance of good information

The number and complexity of issues facing boards requires them to consider very carefully the information they need to fulfil their responsibilities. Too little information prevents the board from engaging fully in the way that it needs to, too much information makes it difficult for boards to highlight the key issues, and they can very easily suffer from overload.

This need for 'intelligent information' is reflected in *The Intelligent Board*, produced by the independent research and analysis body, Dr Foster, in conjunction with The Appointments Commission.

In proposing a number of principles for board reporting, as well as providing a framework for strategic issues and operational performance, 'the key tests of the success of any information resource for the board will be the extent to which it:

- prompts relevant and constructive challenge
- supports informed decision-making
- is effective in providing early warning of potential financial or other problems
- develops all directors' understanding of the organisation and its performance.'

Information – good practice tip

It is a truism to say that the NHS is data rich, but information poor. Too often organisations work with the information that is available, often for historical reasons, rather than the information that is needed. In addition many organisations are good at measuring their inputs and processes, but less capable of assessing and evaluating the outcomes.

Good governance is about good decision-making, and good decisions can be made only with good information. Boards should spend time thinking about the information that they want and need, how it is to be presented and, to a certain extent, the information that they do not need. A good question to ask is 'what does any particular report provide?' If it does not provide assurance that systems are working or performance is on target, or if it does not prompt any action to make sure systems do work or performance is satisfactory, then why are you looking at it? There is no value in having 'fancy that' information.

Key questions for the organisation to consider

1. Does our induction programme make clear how accountability flows through the NHS and where our organisation sits?
2. Are roles and responsibilities of our board and its committees clear and understood?
3. Do we review the committee structure regularly and ensure that each element adds value?
4. Does our board:
   - share collective responsibility for adding value to the organisation – promoting the organisation's success and directing and supervising its affairs
   - provide leadership within a framework of prudent and effective control which enables risk to be assessed and managed
   - look ahead – setting the strategic vision and challenging/approving the aims/objectives set by the chief executive
   - set and maintain organisational tone, culture and values?
5. Does our organisation foster and encourage constructive challenge at all levels?
6. Do we understand the priorities facing the organisation and receive sufficient information in the right format and at the right time to make a judgement on the management of the agenda?
7. Are the roles and responsibilities of the organisation's audit committee, remuneration committee and (in the case of PCTs) professional executive committee clear? If so, do we receive effective advice and feedback from each committee?
8. Are charitable funds managed by a dedicated committee that is NOT a board committee? Do we understand that charitable funds are separate from NHS monies and that they are governed by charity law and the Charity Commission's regulatory regime?
9. Does our chief executive:
   - help the board project a clear vision for the organisation
   - provide information and expertise to the board
   - provide operational leadership
   - provide effective control systems
   - deliver against operational objectives?
10. Does our organisation's board:
    - support the management of the organisation
    - set demanding but realisable operational objectives
    - challenge and thereby reinforce the effectiveness of control systems
    - support the chief executive in making changes and taking risks by corporately agreeing plans and strategies and taking corporate responsibility for outcomes
    - establish a forward thinking, modernising, high quality and patient-focused culture for the organisation?
11. Do the organisation's structures and committees allow all important matters to be addressed at an appropriate level? Do we know what the appropriate levels are? What is the escalation process? Do committees tend to compartmentalise problems and decisions? Or do they enable all aspects of key issues to be taken into account in an integrated manner (for example, clinical, financial, structural etc.)? What examples do we have of decisions and plans that take effective account of all aspects? What examples do we have of poor decisions or plans that did not take account of all aspects?

12. Do we have clear structures, processes and accountabilities in place for partnership working? How do we assess their effectiveness?
13. Do we have a clear understanding of governance arrangements for outsourced services? In particular do we know what risks the organisation has retained?

This chapter's main learning points

- In all NHS organisations there needs to be absolute clarity about who is responsible for what
- The board is the pre-eminent governing body and is responsible for the strategies and actions of its organisation
- There is a range of responsibilities and decisions that boards cannot delegate
- At present (2011/12), every NHS organisation must have an audit committee and a remuneration committee that report to the board. Primary care trusts must have a professional executive committee
- Every NHS organisation has an accountable officer who is the chief executive – this will also apply as the NHSCB and clinical commissioning groups
- Chief executives are accountable to the board for meeting its objectives, day to day management and ensuring effective governance arrangements
- Chief executives are accountable to the Secretary of State or Monitor for stewardship of public funds and the organisation's performance
- Governance structures operating in silos are not effective – there needs to be an integrated approach
- Governance structures come under particular pressure when services are provided in partnership or outsourced
- Mergers and re-organisations challenge governance structures and threaten business continuity
- The success of governance structures and effectiveness of the board depends on the quality of information available.

Further reading

Government response to the NHS Future Forum, 2011:
www.dh.gov.uk/en/Publicationsandstatistics/Publications/PublicationsPolicyAndGuidance/DH_127444

Your Statutory Duties: a Reference Guide for NHS Foundation Trust Governors, Monitor, 2009:
www.monitor-nhsft.gov.uk/home/our-publications/browse-category/guidance-foundation-trusts/reports/guidance-governors/your-sta

The Healthy NHS Board: principles for good governance, National Leadership Council Report:
www.nhsleadership.org.uk/

NHS Foundation Trust Code of Governance, Monitor:
www.monitor-nhsft.gov.uk/home/our-publications/browse-category/guidance-foundation-trusts/mandatory-guidance/code-governance-

The Higgs Report on the Role and Effectiveness of NEDs, 2003:
www.icaew.com/en/library/subject-gateways/corporate-governance/codes-and-reports

Governing the NHS: a Guide for NHS Boards, NHS Appointments Commission, 2003:
www.dh.gov.uk/en/Publicationsandstatistics/Publications/PublicationsPolicyAndGuidance/DH_4082638

The Committee on Standards in Public Life: www.public-standards.gov.uk/

NHS Audit Committee Handbook, HFMA, 2011: www.hfma.org.uk/publications-and-guidance/

NHS Act 2006: www.legislation.gov.uk/ukpga/2006/41/contents

NHS Charitable Funds: a Practical Guide, HFMA, 2008:
www.hfma.org.uk/publications-and-guidance/

Accounting Officer Memorandum, Monitor:
www.monitor-nhsft.gov.uk/home/our-publications/browse-category/guidance-foundation-trusts/mandatory-guidance/revised-nhs-foun

Managing Public Money, HM Treasury: www.hm-treasury.gov.uk/psr_mpm_index.htm

The Role of the Finance Director in a Patient-led NHS – A Guide for NHS Boards, Finance Staff Development Board:
www.fsdnetwork.com/documents/roleofdf.pdf

HFMA Policy Statement on the Role of the NHS Finance Director:
www.hfma.org.uk/publications-and-guidance/

The Integrated Governance Handbook, Department of Health, 2006:
www.dh.gov.uk/en/Publicationsandstatistics/Publications/PublicationsPolicyAndGuidance/DH_4128739

Integrated Governance: a guide to risk and joining up the NHS reforms, HFMA, 2011:
www.hfma.org.uk/publications-and-guidance/

Hitting the Fast Lane: Driving Long-term Integration in NHS Mergers, HFMA, 2006:
www.hfma.org.uk/publications-and-guidance/

The Intelligent Board, Dr Foster in conjunction with the Appointments Commission:
www.drfosterhealth.co.uk/features/commissioning-to-reduce-inequalities/

Chapter 6: Internal Systems and Processes: Statutory Requirements

Introduction

As well as ensuring that your organisation's structure is in line with statutory requirements and that boards are able to monitor, respond and adhere to legislative and regulatory developments, the delivery of healthcare depends on effective internal procedures and controls. In the NHS there are a number of statutory requirements that organisations and their boards need to fulfil in this context. This chapter looks first at accountability requirements and the formal guidance that underpins these and then goes on to the board's assurance framework and performance management, monitoring and reporting. Throughout, the focus is on how things stand under the current regime – i.e. prior to the implementation of the coalition government's reforms. The extent to which internal systems and processes will be set down in statute for the new clinical commissioning groups is not yet clear but it is assumed that there will be some minimum requirements that will be broadly similar to those currently in place.

Accountability

The Department of Health's *Code of Accountability for NHS Boards* sets out the basis on which strategic health authorities (SHAs), primary care trusts (PCTs) and NHS trusts should fulfil their duties and responsibilities (see chapter 3). Amongst other things, this Code emphasises that:

- board members collectively share corporate responsibility for all board decisions
- there is a clear division of responsibility between the board's chair and the organisation's chief executive – the chief executive is accountable to the board for meeting their objectives and to the NHS chief executive for the organisation's performance (see chapter 5 for more on the role of the accountable officer)
- the board is required to 'meet regularly and retain full and effective control over the organisation'
- the chair and NEDs are responsible for monitoring the organisation's executive management
- boards' standing orders should 'prescribe the terms on which committees and sub-committees of the board may be delegated functions and should include the schedule of decisions reserved for the board'
- boards must 'present through the timely publication of an annual report, annual accounts and other means, a balanced assessment of the organisation's performance'.

Although the *Code of Accountability* does not apply to foundation trusts (FTs), they too must make clear how they intend to go about achieving their objectives and duties. FTs' powers are set out in their constitutions and standing orders for boards of governors and boards of directors are embedded in these documents – see chapter 9 and Monitor's website for more details.

As we saw in chapter 3, it is not yet known whether or not the *Code of Accountability* will continue to apply under the new regime.

Business rules

Standing orders

At present all NHS organisations have their own business rules that must include standing orders (SOs). These SOs provide a comprehensive framework for carrying out activities and are therefore a critical element in the governance framework. For SHAs, PCTs and NHS trusts, SOs are the link to an organisation's statutory powers and translate these powers into a series of practical rules designed to protect the interests of both the organisation and its staff. In many ways SOs are similar to the memorandum and articles of association of a company.

The majority of provisions within SOs set out the rules by which the board, and its committees, will conduct their business, including:

- the composition of the board and committees
- how meetings are run
- form, content and frequency of reports submitted to the board
- what constitutes a quorum
- record of attendance
- voting procedures
- appointment of committees and sub–committees.

SOs also set out the duties and obligations of board members and the standards they are expected to adhere to. Two areas worthy of particular attention are:

- scheme of delegation and decisions reserved to the board
- standards of business conduct including declarations of interest and hospitality.

Reservation and delegation of powers

A key aim of SOs is to make clear who is responsible for decision taking. To that end, SHAs, PCTs and NHS trusts must include within their SOs a schedule of decisions reserved to the board and a scheme of delegation to other committees or officers. This is a detailed listing of what the board alone can decide upon and who the board empowers to take actions or make decisions on its behalf. This is an important statement of where authority lies within the organisation and must be treated as a 'living' or working document that is subject to regular review, at least annually.

Examples of decisions reserved to the board include:

- approving the standing orders
- establishing terms of reference and reporting arrangements for all committees
- agreeing the schedule of reserved decisions and scheme of delegation
- approving standing financial instructions – these set out detailed procedures and responsibilities in relation to financial aspects (see later in this chapter for more detail)
- appointing the board's vice chair
- defining the organisation's strategic aims

- approving business cases for capital investment
- approving budgets
- receiving and approving the annual report and annual accounts.

If for any reason the person authorised to take a decision (as set out in the scheme of delegation) is not available responsibility should ideally go up the hierarchy, rather than down.

FTs include details about decisions reserved to the board and a scheme of delegation within their SOs which form part of their constitution.

Standards of business conduct

One area covered by SOs that often receives particular attention relates to standards of business conduct, declarations of interest and hospitality. The fact that this is deliberately included in SOs rather than delegated to standing financial instructions (SFIs) indicates to managers and staff how important it is to follow the procedures set down and the importance attributed to probity.

The need for effective rules in this area has been further heightened by the *Bribery Act 2010* which came into effect on 1 July 2011and repeals all existing anti-bribery and anti-corruption legislation. The Act applies to both organisations and individuals and creates four distinct offences:

- bribing another person
- receiving a bribe
- bribing a foreign official
- failure to prevent bribery.

NHS bodies need to ensure that they have in place adequate procedures to prevent bribery taking place as they can be prosecuted for failing to prevent a bribe being paid on the organisation's behalf (for example when placing a contract for a major service or investment). Similarly, the Act will be relevant in relation to corporate hospitality so organisations need to ensure that they have procedures to prevent misconduct.

On **declarations of interest**, the *Code of Accountability* requires chairs and board directors to declare any personal or business interests that may 'influence (or be perceived to influence) their judgement'. The fundamental principle is that no one should use their public position for private gain, either for their own benefit or for the benefit of those close to them. For example, if a board/committee member or officer has any interest in a contract, that interest must be disclosed and they must take no part in the evaluation process or decision. It is important that both actual and potential conflicts of interest are declared as any outside interest, hospitality or sponsorship represents a risk of a conflict arising. It is also an offence to accept gifts or hospitality as an inducement or reward for doing something in your public role and staff are advised to refuse to accept such gifts or hospitality rather than declare subsequent to the event. There is some leeway for minor gifts (for example, pens or diaries) but the offer of higher value items should be questioned.

The key point here is that board, committee members and staff must be open about any gifts they have received or been offered. A good test is to think about how it would look on the front page of the local newspaper: if the action or gift could not be defended then it should not be carried out or accepted.

Model SOs (including schemes of delegation) for SHAs, NHS Trusts and PCTs were issued in March 2006 and are available from the Department of Health's website.

Standing financial instructions

SFIs are designed to ensure that NHS organisations account fully and openly for all that they do. The areas covered include:

- the role of audit
- business planning
- budgets, budgetary control and monitoring
- annual accounts and reports
- banking arrangements
- tendering and contracting procedures
- commissioning
- income, fees and charges
- service agreements with other NHS organisations
- terms of service and payment of staff
- non pay expenditure
- capital investment
- external borrowing
- security of assets
- disposals and condemnations, losses and special payments
- retention of records
- patients' property
- risk management and insurance
- funds held on trust.

SFIs tend to be fairly prescriptive and although all directors, managers and staff need to be aware of them, they are generally of most relevance to decision makers and budget holders. The key issues for budget holders tend to be around the authorisation of expenditure, control of monies due and budgetary control. An effective approach to governance will involve ensuring that budget holders and managers are regularly trained in these areas and supported by finance and audit staff who make clear why controls are important.

Tendering and contracting procedures need particular attention – it is important that when tendering for contracts and services the overriding objective is to get best value from a 'fair and adequate' competitive process. Organisations can set their own financial limits for different procedures but the basic principle should be that as the value of the contract increases, so should the rigour of the process. This can range from competitive quotations for lower value orders to a full and detailed tendering process under EU directives governing public procurement.

Model SFIs for SHAs, PCTs and NHS trusts are available on the Department of Health's website. Many organisations inform their staff of the agreed SOs and SFIs using their intranet sites, supplemented by summarised handbooks and presentations on key points.

FTs do not have to have SFIs – however, many do use them and others have written financial procedures that fulfil the same function.

Compliance

It is essential that all board, committee members and staff are aware of the organisation's SOs and SFIs and adhere to them. A deliberate breach can result in summary dismissal – for example this could be the end result if a contract were let to a company that a board member had an interest in without following tendering rules or declaring an interest.

Although a formal waiver of SOs is possible it must be approved in advance, usually by the chief executive, and the reasons set down in a permanent record. For example, tendering procedures may be waived under certain circumstances provided that there are valid reasons that will withstand objective scrutiny and that the approach complies with both UK and EU law. A failure to agree a waiver in advance can be deemed to be a breach of SOs, which can lead to disciplinary action.

Although there is no detailed guidance in this area, it is assumed that all NHS organisations under the new regime will need to have in place 'business rules' of some sort that fulfil the same function as SOs, schemes of delegation and SFIs.

Basic documentation – good practice tip

At the inception of any new organisation, and periodically in subsequent years, organisations will adopt their governance framework documents – standing orders, standing financial instructions, reservation of powers to the board, scheme of delegation, codes of conduct, accountability and openness, etc.

This documentation is weighty, but necessary and yet is often not read by board members. It is important to recognise that these documents set out the fundamentals of how an organisation wishes to be run and should not gather dust on a shelf.

One of the main documents from a board's perspective is the reservation of powers to the board, which sets out what the board has said that it and it alone should deal with, in terms of decision-making and reporting. This should be a live document that is reviewed, at least annually, and amended to reflect the wishes and needs of board members.

Realism is needed in all this documentation. It is all too easy to take the model documents from the Department of Health website, run a quick 'edit and replace' to put the organisation's name in then get the board to adopt them at the end of a four hour meeting. This might 'tick' the box, but does not create effective documentation overnight.

Boards should spend some time thinking about how they want to govern their organisations and then use the governance documentation to support this.

One way of making governance documentation more accessible is to use an intranet that allows managers and staff to interact with the content and includes (for example) questions and answers or FAQs.

Internal control

To be able to satisfy requirements set by government and others and to meet their own objectives, organisations must have effective internal systems and processes. The purpose of an internal control system is to minimise the risk of an organisation not achieving its objectives. The accountable officer is responsible for maintaining it. An internal control system must:

- identify and prioritise the risks to the achievement of the organisation's objectives
- evaluate the likelihood of those risks being realised and the consequent impact
- manage the risks efficiently, effectively and economically.

At present, all NHS organisations have such a system – in future, for a clinical commissioning group, the key strategic objective will be something like 'to secure the best value and quality of care for the population they serve whilst also promoting health and well being'. At the core of an effective internal control system there needs to be a structured approach to identifying objectives, risks and problem areas. In the NHS this structure is currently provided by an 'assurance framework' or 'board assurance framework' underpinned by a risk management system.

Assurance framework

Under the current regime, SHAs, PCTs and NHS trusts are required to have in place an assurance framework[1] that must be approved by the board. An assurance framework provides organisations with a simple but comprehensive method for the effective and focussed management of the principal risks to meeting their objectives and the associated assurances. FTs are not required to develop an assurance framework but it is considered best practice.

The assurance framework is used to determine the core of the board agenda and focus attention on the biggest risks and how those risks are to be minimised so that objectives are not compromised.

Chapter 7 explains risk management and the assurance framework in more depth and there is a wealth of guidance in the *NHS Audit Committee Handbook*.

---

[1] *Building the Assurance Framework: a practical guide for NHS boards*, Department of Health, 2003.

Performance management and monitoring – external influences

Government policy and strategy

The most significant external influence for all NHS organisations is central government policy. Since the NHS Plan was published in 2000, a series of policy statements have been issued setting out the overall strategic direction for the NHS and its key priorities. For example, in 2005, *Creating a Patient Led NHS* set out four key strategic strands:

- more choice and a much stronger voice for patients
- more diverse providers, with more freedom to innovate and challenge poor performance
- money following the patients, rewarding the best and most efficient and giving the others a real incentive to improve
- a framework of regulation and decision-making that guarantees quality, fairness, equity and value for money.

In 2007, the labour government asked then health minister Lord Darzi to carry out a review of the NHS. His final report *High Quality Care for all: NHS Next Stage Review* was issued in 2008 and set out a vision of an NHS that 'gives patients and the public more information and choice, works in partnership and has quality of care at its heart'.

This focus on quality remains at the heart of the coalition government's approach to the NHS – its 2010 white paper, *Equity and Excellence: Liberating the NHS* made this clear in the foreword when it stated that:

- 'patients will be at the heart of everything we do. So they will have more choice and control, helped by easy access to the information they need about the best GPs and hospitals. Patients will be in charge of making decisions about their care'
- 'there will be a relentless focus on clinical outcomes. Success will be measured, not through bureaucratic process targets, but against results that really matter to patients – such as improving cancer and stroke survival rates'
- 'we will empower health professionals. Doctors and nurses must be able to use their professional judgement about what is right for patients. We will support this by giving frontline staff more control. Healthcare will be run from the bottom up, with ownership and decision-making in the hands of professionals and patients'.

Operating frameworks

Implementation of government priorities across the NHS is guided by the Department of Health's NHS *Operating Framework*, which is used by NHS organisations at every level when planning their own activities for the coming period. In the case of FTs, Monitor incorporates the main provisions of the *Operating Framework* in its own *Compliance Framework*. An *Operating Framework* is issued annually and provides both a structure and specific priorities for planning across the NHS. The structure requires each organisation to draw up its own operational plan – at present this involves:

- PCTs drawing up plans that address the needs of their local community and reflect national priorities

- NHS trusts developing plans that show how resources will be used to deliver national and local priorities and fit with PCT plans
- SHAs bringing together PCT plans to form a comprehensive operational plan for their area.

Local plans are treated as 'live' documents that are monitored regularly at local level and updated as new initiatives come up or problems are encountered. SHAs also use these plans as the basis for monitoring and assessing performance.

The *Operating Framework* provides guidance on how commissioners and providers should work together, using the available mechanisms (for example, contracting and tariff arrangements) to bring about change in line with the national priorities.

The overall priorities in the *Operating Framework 2011/12* are consistent with previous years but also cover transitional issues as the NHS prepares for the coalition government'sreforms. There is also a series of indicators and milestones that are used for planning and assessing delivery of PCT and SHA plans grouped under three domains:

- quality (safety, effectiveness and experience)
- resources (finance, workforce, capacity and activity)
- reform (commissioning, provision, partnership building, putting patients first and developing the new public health infrastructure).

For full details see the Department's website.

Care Quality Commission

The CQC is responsible for (amongst other activities) operating a registration system that applies to all health and adult social care providers, as set out in regulations under the *Health and Social Care Act 2008* (the *Health and Social Care Act 2008 (Regulated Activities) Regulations 2009*). See chapter 4 for more details.

Local authorities

Since January 2003, overview and scrutiny committees set up by local authorities with social services responsibilities have been empowered to scrutinise health services in their areas. Boards of NHS organisations need to ensure that arrangements are in place to discharge these responsibilities.

Local authority overview and scrutiny powers will continue under the coalition government's new regime but local authorities will have a stronger role in supporting patient choice, ensuring local involvement and leading on health improvement and reducing health inequalities. In particular, they will lead the joint strategic needs assessment (at present this a joint responsibility with PCTs), via newly established health and wellbeing boards which will have a duty to involve users and the public. These health and wellbeing boards will also work with new clinical commissioning groups to ensure that commissioning plans meet local needs. This approach is designed to provide strategic co-ordination to the commissioning of NHS services, social care and health improvement. Members of clinical commissioning groups will be represented on the health and wellbeing boards. Local authorities will jointly commission some services with commissioning groups and will appoint a Director of Public Health in conjunction with the newly established Public Health Service – Public Health England.

Patient and community representatives

Since January 2003, NHS trusts, PCTs and SHAs have been under a statutory duty to make arrangements to involve patients and the public in service planning and operation, and in the development of proposals for changes. This duty is now set out in Section 242 of the consolidated *NHS Act 2006*. To help NHS organisations fulfil this requirement, the Department of Health has issued *Real involvement: working with people to improve healthcare* which is available on its website.

Patient and public engagement – objectives

- To offer world-class, patient-centred health and social care for everyone
- To use patient experience to improve service quality
- To positively engage and empower everyone through shared knowledge, activities, outcomes and best practice.

Source: Helping the NHS put patients at the heart of care, Department of Health, 2009.

Since April 2008 this approach has been supplemented by Local Involvement Networks (LINks), which are made up of local individuals and community groups. Their role is to find out what local people think about local health and social care services and publicly-funded services are required to respond to any suggestions they make. Under the coalition government's planned changes, local HealthWatch will take over from LINks but with the same basic remit – to ensure that the views of patients, carers and the public are taken into account. Local HealthWatch will be funded directly by local authorities. It will receive direction, leadership and support from HealthWatch England, an independent committee within the CQC and set up to be a 'consumer champion'.

NHS Litigation Authority

The NHS Litigation Authority is a special health authority that was established to administer schemes under which NHS bodies could pool their clinical negligence liabilities and to promote high standards of risk management.

The best known scheme is the Clinical Negligence Scheme for Trusts (CNST) – although this is a voluntary membership scheme all NHS trusts, FTs and PCTs in England currently belong. It covers all clinical claims where the incident took place on or after 1 April 1995. The costs of meeting these claims are met through members' contributions on a 'pay-as-you-go' basis.

To be a member of the scheme an organisation must comply with NHSLA standards which are recognised as best practice.

NHS Protect

The NHS Business Services Authority has set up NHS Protect which 'leads on work to identify and tackle crime across the health service'. Its aim is 'to protect NHS staff and resources from activities that would otherwise undermine their effectiveness and their ability to meet the needs of patients and professionals. Ultimately, this helps to ensure the proper use of valuable NHS resources and a safer, more secure environment in which to deliver and receive care.'[2]

Its objectives are to:

- educate and inform those who work for or use the NHS about crime in the health service and how to tackle it
- prevent and deter crime in the NHS by removing opportunities for it to occur or to re-occur
- hold to account those who have committed crime against the NHS by detecting and prosecuting offenders and seeking redress where viable.

Although there are no specific statutory requirements in relation to NHS organisations the expectation is that they will deliver the national NHS Protect strategy at local level. For more information see NHS Protect's website.

Performance management and monitoring – internal systems

Annual accounts

All NHS bodies have a statutory duty to produce annual accounts. For NHS trusts, PCTs and SHAs, the relevant legislation is section 232 and paragraph 3(1) of schedule 15 of the NHS Act 2006 and for FTs, section 30 and paragraph 25(1) of schedule 7 of the NHS Act 2006. The form and content of the accounts is prescribed by the Secretary of State for Health or Monitor for FTs. The production of the statutory annual accounts is the principal means by which NHS bodies discharge their accountability to taxpayers and users of services for their stewardship of public money.

The annual financial statements must also include a statement setting out the responsibilities of directors, a Statement on Internal Control (SIC) and a Quality Account (see below).

Annual reports

The annual report is primarily a narrative document similar to the directors' report described in the Companies Act, but with additional information reflecting the NHS organisation's position

---

[2] NHS Protect website.

in the community. It gives an account of the organisation's activities and performance in the financial year and must include audited accounts/summary financial statements. The annual report must be approved by the board and presented at a public meeting held before 30 September following the end of the relevant financial year. Although the layout of the annual report is not prescribed, the Department of Health's manuals for accounts specify the areas that should be covered – these are Companies Act requirements which apply to NHS bodies

Quality accounts

Since 2010 providers of NHS healthcare have been required to publish a Quality Account, as set out in *High Quality Care for All*. The Quality Account is an annual report to the public on the quality of healthcare services the organisation delivers, with the aim of improving public accountability. The intention is that the public, patients and others with an interest will use a Quality Account to understand:

- what an organisation is doing well
- where improvements in service quality are required
- what the organisation's priorities for improvement are for the coming year
- how the organisation has involved people who use their services, staff and others in determining these priorities.

Prior to publication, providers are expected to share their Quality Account with local commissioning PCTs, the appropriate LINk (in future, local HealthWatch) and the appropriate local authority overview and scrutiny committee.

Statement on Internal Control

The chief executive of an NHS body, as accountable officer, has a statutory responsibility to prepare a Statement on Internal Control (SIC) each year. This includes FTs where it is known as the annual governance statement. Accountable officers are required to provide assurance about the effectiveness of their system of internal control and demonstrate that they are doing their reasonable best to manage the principal risks to the organisation achieving its objectives and to identify any significant weaknesses which need to be addressed. The assurance framework provides evidence to support the SIC. See chapter 7 for more details.

Head of Internal Audit Opinion

A Head of Internal Audit Opinion must be provided annually to support the SIC and inform and comment on the adequacy of the assurance framework. This opinion is based on a combination of the assurance work that internal audit does throughout the year (as set out in the annual audit plan) and their assessment of the overall arrangements for obtaining assurance. Internal auditors typically use four assurance levels when providing assurance opinions:

- **full (or 'high') assurance**: the system of internal control is sound and controls are consistently applied in all the areas reviewed

- **significant assurance**: there is a generally sound system of control. However, some weaknesses in the design or inconsistent application of controls put the achievement of a particular objective at risk
- **limited assurance**: there are weaknesses in the design or inconsistent application of controls that mean objectives are at risk
- **no assurance**: there are weaknesses in control or consistent non-compliance with key controls that could result in failure to achieve objectives.

Other policies and procedures

For NHS bodies to run smoothly, many more policies and procedures (both financial and non-financial) are required. These are usually pulled together in organisational policy and procedure manuals. These cover a wide variety of areas including operational policies (for example, financial procedures issued by the director of finance and nursing policies/procedures issued by the director of nursing) to health and safety and equal opportunities policies and, critically for good governance, policies on how to deal with complaints, clinical negligence claims and freedom of information requests. There should also be a whistle blowing policy, to ensure that concerns raised by staff and other stakeholders are taken seriously, without adverse consequences for the person raising that concern. The relevant legislation for whistle blowing is the *Public Interest Disclosure Act 1998*.

Key questions for the organisation to consider

1. Does everyone in the organisation understand that whilst the board is the pre-eminent governing body, all staff play a role in ensuring effective governance?
2. Is the organisation achieving its objectives?
3. Are the roles of the chair and chief executive clearly distinguished and understood by board members? Are these roles respected by the incumbents? Do they fulfil their respective roles effectively?
4. Do we clearly understand which powers and decisions are reserved to the board? If so, do these include:
   - financial stewardship responsibilities, including adopting the annual report and accounts
   - setting its strategic direction and approving the organisation's strategy and policies
   - appointing senior executives
   - overseeing the delivery of services
   - standards of governance and behaviour?
5. Does the organisation maintain a meaningful set of standing orders, which is reviewed and renewed on a regular basis? Do the SOs facilitate the effective conduct of business by the board? Are all board members and staff aware of the SOs and are they adhered to? How do we test that this is the case?
6. Does the organisation maintain a scheme of delegation, including powers reserved to the board, which is reviewed and renewed on a regular basis? Does this scheme facilitate the effective and appropriate conduct of business by the organisation? Are all board members and staff aware of the scheme and is it adhered to? How do we test that this is the case?

7. Are our rules on declarations of interest and hospitality clear and unambiguous? Are they known, understood and followed by the board and all staff?
8. Do we have adequate procedures in place to prevent bribery in line with the 2010 Act?
9. Does the organisation maintain and regularly review its standing financial instructions? Are all board members and staff aware of the SFIs and are they adhered to? How do we test that this is the case?
10. Does the board meet regularly? If so, does the frequency, format and approach to meetings allow the board to 'retain full and effective control over the organisation'?
11. Does each board meeting receive a performance report, which provides an up to date progress report on key strategic objectives and risks previously identified by the board? Do board members have the opportunity to critically challenge the progress made and the evidence that supports it?
12. Does the organisation maintain an assurance framework? Is it fit for purpose and in line with the organisation's main objectives? How is it used? Is the guidance set out in the *NHS Audit Committee Handbook* followed?
13. Does the organisation's operational/business plan meet NHS requirements in terms of structure and the priorities for action? Is the plan realistic and affordable? Will it meet national priorities?
14. How do we ensure that we are aware of policy developments? Do we assess their impact on the organisation?
15. Are we aware of the requirements and expectations of external bodies such as the CQC, local authorities, the NHSLA and NHS Protect?
16. How do we ensure that we meet our statutory duty to involve patients in service planning and proposals for change?
17. Does the board devote sufficient time to reviewing the annual report and accounts, the Quality Account and the SIC?
18. Do we have in place a whistle blowing policy that all staff know about and would feel able to use?
19. Do we regularly review our entire suite of policies and procedures to ensure they remain fit for purpose and up to date?

This chapter's main learning points

- Internal procedures and controls must be effective and in line with statutory requirements
- All boards must draw up standing orders, a schedule of decisions reserved to the board and a scheme of delegation
- SHAs, PCTs and NHS trusts must draw up standing financial instructions
- SHAs, PCTs and NHS trusts must develop an assurance framework that drives the board agenda
- All NHS provider organisations must be registered with the CQC
- NHS trusts, PCTs and SHAs must involve and consult patients and the public

- All NHS bodies must prepare annual reports and audited accounts, a Quality Account and a SIC
- All NHS organisations must draw up local plans that reflect both local and national priorities and targets
- All NHS organisations should have a whistle blowing policy.

Further reading

The Department of Health and NHS Appointments Commission Code of Conduct: Code of Accountability in the NHS for NHS Boards, 2004:
www.dh.gov.uk/en/Publicationsandstatistics/Publications/PublicationsPolicyAndGuidance/DH_4116281

Monitor: www.monitor-nhsft.gov.uk

Standards of business conduct for NHS staff HSG (93) 5 – available from the health service guidelines pages of the Department of Health website:
www.dh.gov.uk/en/Publicationsandstatistics/Lettersandcirculars/Healthserviceguidelines/DH_4017845

Model standing orders, reservation and delegation of powers and standing financial instructions for SHAs, PCTs and NHS trusts, Department of Health, 2006:
www.dh.gov.uk/en/Publicationsandstatistics/Publications/PublicationsPolicyAndGuidance/DH_4132059

Building the assurance framework: a practical guide for NHS Boards, Department of Health, 2003:
www.dh.gov.uk/en/Managingyourorganisation/Workforce/Leadership/Governance/index.htm

Creating a Patient Led NHS: Delivering the NHS Improvement Plan, Department of Health, 2005:
www.dh.gov.uk/en/Publicationsandstatistics/Publications/PublicationsPolicyAndGuidance/DH_4106506

High Quality Care for all: NHS Next Stage Review final report, Department of Health, 2008:
www.dh.gov.uk/en/Publicationsandstatistics/Publications/PublicationsPolicyAndGuidance/DH_085825

NHS Operating Framework, Department of Health:
www.dh.gov.uk/en/Publicationsandstatistics/Publications/PublicationsPolicyAndGuidance/DH_122738

Compliance Framework, Monitor:
www.monitor-nhsft.gov.uk/home/our-publications/browse-category/guidance-foundation-trusts/mandatory-guidance/compliance-frame-0

Health and Social Care Act 2008 (Registration of Regulated Activities) Regulations, 2009:
www.opsi.gov.uk/si/si2009/uksi_20090660_en_1

NHS Protect: www.nhsbsa.nhs.uk/Protect.aspx

NHS Act 2006: www.legislation.gov.uk/ukpga/2006/41/contents

Real involvement: working with people to improve healthcare, Department of Health, 2008: www.dh.gov.uk/en/Publicationsandstatistics/Publications/PublicationsPolicyAndGuidance/DH_089787

Chapter 7: Risk Management and the Assurance Framework

Introduction

So far this guide has focused on the need to have the right leadership and management structures in place to enable an organisation to pursue its objectives whilst adhering to legislative and regulatory requirements. This is an important element of good governance but organisations also need to ensure that their system of internal control is operating in a way that is effective in ensuring the delivery of objectives by focusing on minimising risk.

This chapter looks at how this can be achieved through the development of an effective and comprehensive assurance framework, tailored to suit the organisation's local circumstances.

Accountabilities

As we saw in chapter 6, the accountable (or accounting in FTs) officer is responsible for maintaining a sound system of internal control that supports the achievement of the organisation's strategic objectives. The Audit Commission's 2009 guide, *Taking it on Trust* defines internal control as 'the process that provides assurance that an organisation is achieving its objectives and meeting its legal and other obligations. It includes the governance framework, risk management, information and communications, monitoring processes and assurance activities. It is the effectiveness of all this that the accountable officer is certifying when signing the Statement on Internal Control (SIC).' The system of internal control must therefore be an ongoing process designed to:

- identify and prioritise the risks to the achievement of these objectives
- evaluate the likelihood of those risks being realised and the consequent impact
- manage the risk efficiently, effectively and economically.

In practice, this means that at the core of an effective internal control system there needs to be a structured approach to identifying objectives, risks and problem areas. In the NHS this structure is currently provided by an 'assurance framework' underpinned by a risk management system.

The assurance framework

The *NHS Audit Committee Handbook* describes the assurance framework as 'the key source of evidence that links strategic objectives to risks, controls and assurances, and the main tool that the board should use in discharging its overall responsibility for internal control'. The Handbook contains detailed practical guidance on how to use the framework to best effect.

It is important to emphasise that there is no single template for an assurance framework – each board should make its own decisions about the format based on a sound understanding of the principal risks that could prevent the organisation achieving its agreed objectives and the potential effect each risk could have on those objectives. However, *Building the Assurance Framework: a Practical Guide for NHS Boards*, issued by the Department in 2003 defines the essential components, as follows:

- establish strategic objectives
- identify the principal risks that may threaten the achievement of these objectives
- identify, and evaluate the design of key controls intended to manage these principal risks
- identify the arrangements for obtaining assurance on the effectiveness of these key controls
- evaluate the reliability of the assurances identified
- identify positive assurances and areas where there are gaps in controls and/or assurances
- put in place plans to take corrective action where gaps have been identified in relation to principal risks
- maintain dynamic risk management arrangements including, crucially, a well-founded risk register.

To be effective, each of these aspects must be painstakingly considered and regularly reviewed and updated. Board members should not be afraid of asking searching questions such as 'are we meeting our stated objectives for delivering high quality healthcare?' and if so 'what evidence is there?'

The setting of strategic objectives is fundamental to the identification of which risks are most significant to the board. It is important that the board's assurance framework reports only on principal (or most significant) risks so that its considerations are focussed on the key areas. The Audit Commission's definition is helpful here: 'Strategic risks are those that represent major threats to achieving the trust's strategic objectives or to its continued existence. Strategic risks will include key operational service failures.'[1]

> **Practical example – review of strategic objectives**
>
> This trust's audit committee holds a workshop to review the initial assurance framework for the year, following the board's approval of the corporate strategic objectives. About six months later, a mid-year review takes place to help ensure that any new risks arising have been appropriately included in the assurance framework.

Having established key objectives and the risks that threaten their achievement the next stage is to identify controls that will mitigate their likelihood or impact (or both). However, it is not enough simply to record these controls, however well-designed they might be. It is also vitally important that the board deals with areas where there are gaps in control and gaps in assurance. The board will want to hold the executive to account in dealing with these and to ensure there is an action plan to fill such gaps.

One of the biggest mistakes boards make is in devoting insufficient attention to the quality of assurances. Placing reliance on well-designed controls that are not working can cause major upsets and embarrassment to boards. If there is no assurance that controls are working the risk presented by each exposure reverts to intrinsic levels – in other words, it is uncontrolled.

---

[1] *Taking it on Trust*, Audit Commission 2009.

The board should look closely at the assurances provided and distinguish those that are positive (i.e. confirm a control is effective) from those that are negative (i.e. a control is not working or is ineffective). In the latter case, the board must look for action to rectify the problem.

In reviewing the assurances, the board should also consider how reliable the source and nature of each assurance is (for example, how independent, how rigorous, how current). The *NHS Audit Committee Handbook* contains more detail on suggested criteria for assessing assurances and boards may look to their audit committee to perform this scrutiny. The table below gives an indication of sources of assurance that are commonly used by NHS boards:

Commonly used sources of assurance	
Internal sources of assurance	**External sources of assurance**
Internal audit	External audit
Key performance indicators	Audit Commission
Performance reports	NHS Litigation Authority/clinical negligence
Sub-committee reports	scheme for trusts
Compliance audit reports	Strategic health authority reports/reviews
Local counter fraud work	Monitor
Clinical audit	Care Quality Commission hygiene code
Staff satisfaction surveys	reports
Staff appraisals	Care Quality Commission reviews
Training records	Care Quality Commission registration
Training evaluation reports	reviews
Results of internal investigations	Royal College visits
Serious untoward incident reports	Deanery visits
Complaints records	External benchmarking
Infection control reports	Patient environment action team reports
Declarations to Care Quality Commission	Accreditation schemes
Information governance toolkit	National and regional audits
self-assessment	Peer reviews
Patient advice and liaison services reports	Feedback from service users
Human resource reports	Feedback from commissioners
Internal benchmarking	External advisors
Clinical coding reports	Local networks (e.g. cancer networks)
Estates strategy	Investors in People
Project board minutes (for major projects)	National Patient Safety Agency reports
Research outputs	Information Commissioner
Information governance reports	National Confidential Enquiry into Patient Outcome and Death (NCEPOD) reports
Source: adapted from the Audit Commission report *Taking it on Trust*	

Finally, it is always important for boards to look at the big picture to confirm the effectiveness of controls. For example, if assurances say that healthcare is of a high quality but one or more areas are known to have poor outcomes, the board should question what they are being told.

Similarly, the board should be looking to see that their actions are reducing the overall risk level. External reviews (for example by external auditors) will look for evidence that the board has addressed these gaps in control and assurance. Some trusts structure part of their board agenda around issues arising from the assurance framework. Organisations that use their assurance framework in this way and see it as a natural element of their management approach will reap significant benefits.

Although under the coalition government's planned new structure for the NHS, clinical commissioning groups may not be required to have a full formal assurance framework, they will need something similar in place to identify as a minimum:

- the group's principal objectives linked to its business plan – the key objective is likely to be something like 'to secure the best value and quality of care for the population they serve whilst also promoting health and well being'
- key risks to achieving those objectives
- key controls that can manage the risks identified
- independent assurances that risks are being managed and objectives delivered
- gaps in assurance
- gaps in control
- action plans to address the gaps identified.

To give you an idea of what an assurance framework can look like an example that integrates performance and assurance is included as appendix 4. The *Audit Committee Handbook* also includes same example frameworks.

Risk management

As mentioned above, a key element of an effective assurance framework is a sound approach to risk management. Although a lot of jargon has grown up around risk management it is actually something that happens all the time – it is about being aware of potential problems, thinking through what effect they could have and planning ahead to prevent the worst-case scenario. In this context it is important to recognise that no approach to managing risks can give an absolute guarantee that nothing will ever go wrong. It is also worth remembering that risk is about opportunities as well as threats. Good risk management encourages organisations to take well-managed risks that allow safe development, growth and change.

As well as underpinning an organisation's system of internal control and its assurance framework, risk management also plays a key role in the regimes of external regulators such as auditors, the Care Quality Commission and Monitor.

Risk management is now a high profile industry in its own right but the basics are simple. Every organisation needs to have a risk management framework which comprises a 'bottom up' element, for identifying and recording risk and a 'top down' element for stratifying risks, so they can be escalated or delegated to the most appropriate level within the organisation. The basic requirements in any organisation are:

- risk assessment – a generic risk assessment tool to be used for all risks by trained staff at any level
- risk scoring – to quantify and prioritise risks, by scoring the likelihood of an event occurring and the impact on the organisation if it does
- risk treatment – the actions and controls that can reasonably be applied to mitigate or manage a risk
- residual risk – any part of an assessed risk that is not controlled
- risk register – to record in detail the risks faced by the organisation. This should include significant residual risks stratified according to their severity using the risk scores
- risk appetite – the board must define the balance between the cost of mitigating the more severe risks and accepting the less severe risks which are not mitigated. Once decided, this is known as the 'risk appetite' of the organisation. An organisation may also have in place a 'risk tolerance matrix' which documents the severity of residual risk that can be tolerated as determined by the risk appetite
- escalation procedures – having defined the risk appetite, an organisation's risk management framework should also establish the structures and responsibilities for managing all risks and for escalating to a higher level those that are rated above the defined risk appetite.

Good risk management requires leadership and commitment from the top and ownership throughout the organisation. It is not about putting risks in a register and forgetting about them, it is about identifying and managing those risks, particularly those that present the biggest challenge in management terms. These principles are common to all sectors.

In November 2009, the Walker review[2] recommended that a board's risk assessment process should be both qualitative and (as a matter of best practice) involve quantitative metrics to serve as a way of tracking risk management performance in implementation of the organisation's agreed strategy.

To achieve this, staff at all levels need to understand how risks are stratified – in other words, which level of the organisation will be responsible for managing which risks. Using the framework described above, the board's risk appetite statement will set out the level of risk the board will manage. In the same way, risk tolerance levels must be defined for risks that can be managed at lower levels.

Practical example

An organisation might stratify risk at five levels to be managed by the following:

Level 1: individual managers
Level 2: department/speciality
Level 3: directorate
Level 4: executive directors
Level 5: board.

---

[2] The Walker review – *Corporate Governance in Banks and Other Financial Industry Entities*, 2009.

When staff identify a risk they will then know who in the organisation has the delegated responsibility for managing this risk and, if appropriate, escalate the risk or delegate the risk to this person to manage.

Given the importance of risk identification and assessment to the effectiveness of an assurance framework the board also needs to be confident that the organisation's overall approach to risk management is effective and mature. In the first instance the NHSLA standards can be used as a gauge of the level of maturity of the organisation's risk management system. As the organisation's system develops and the NHSLA rating confirms this, supplementary methods of maturity assessment could be considered to identify areas of improvement and help the risk management system to move towards being best practice. HM Treasury and Alarm (the Public Risk Management Association) provide useful assessment tools. The Institute of Internal Auditors (IIA) also sets out a five level maturity framework and a recommended approach to internal auditing at each level of maturity.

Extract from the *Alarm National Performance Model for Risk Management in the Public Services* that identifies five levels of risk maturity

- level 1: risk management is **engaging** with the organisation
- level 2: risk management is **happening** within the organisation
- level 3: risk management is **working** for the organisation
- level 4: risk management is **embedded and integrated** within the organisation
- level 5: risk management is **driving** the organisation

Extract from the IIA's *Position Statement on Risk Based Internal Auditing*

- **risk naive:** no formal approach developed for risk management
- **risk aware:** scattered silo based approach to risk management
- **risk defined:** strategy and policies in place and communicated. Risk appetite defined
- **risk managed:** enterprise wide approach to risk management developed and communicated
- **risk enabled:** risk management and internal control fully embedded into the operations

The application of an appropriate risk management model, the establishment of a process to identify risks, the setting of control standards (such as standing financial instructions) and the use of benchmarking are all risk management techniques.

The benefits of an effective approach to risk management and assurance include:

- reduction in risk exposure through more effective targeting of resources to address key risk areas
- improvements in economy, efficiency and effectiveness resulting from a reduction in the frequency and/or severity of incidents, complaints, claims, staff absence and other loss
- demonstrable compliance with applicable laws and regulations
- enhanced reputation and increased public confidence in the quality of NHS services.

Practical example of a comprehensive risk assurance process

This trust has an effective 'top down, bottom up' approach to the identification and stratification of risk. The 'top down' element is the establishment of a risk stratification (or risk tolerance) matrix which enables it to define clearly its risk appetite. The 'bottom up' is the system whereby every employee may enter risks onto the risk register. These are moderated and classified consistently in accordance with the corporate risk management policy. If the classification ranks them as high in relation to the board's risk appetite, they are escalated to the board's assurance framework.

The assurance framework is formulated in a way which allows the board to focus on key controls and key sources of assurance on all the inherent risks to strategic objectives classified as high. Over each twelve month period the board requires an update from the lead executive director on each of the key controls and key sources of assurance. The strength of these assurances is reviewed by the audit committee annually. Sometimes this review will involve commissioning internal audit to assess the quality of the assurance. In this organisation, a compliance team (which is part of the governance team but is managed by internal audit) ensures that both the key controls and key sources of assurance with respect to all strategic risks are verified during each annual cycle.

National standards and priorities

A key consideration in the overall risk management and assurance framework for the NHS is the need to achieve nationally set standards and priorities designed to underpin the delivery of high quality services. These are set out in policy statements issued by the Department of Health and in its annual *Operating Framework*. Organisations must also fulfil the registration requirements of the Care Quality Commission.

From a governance point of view, organisations need to ensure that their aims sufficiently cover the standards/priorities (i.e. map them to organisational aims and objectives). See chapter 4 for more details about the policy context and Care Quality Commission's regime.

The Statement on Internal Control

The focus on risk management and assurance finds formal expression in the Statement on Internal Control (SIC). Since 2001/02, NHS bodies have had to submit a SIC as part of their annual financial statements. This requirement was set by the Treasury in line with the recommendations in the Turnbull report (see chapter 1). The SIC requires the following disclosures:

- the scope of the accountable officer's responsibility
- the purpose of the system of internal control
- the organisation's capacity to handle risk
- a description of the risk and control framework
- confirmation that a review of effectiveness has been undertaken
- any significant internal control issues.

The SIC must be signed off by the chief executive, as the accountable officer, on behalf of the board. The head of internal audit provides an annual opinion to the accountable officer and the audit committee on the adequacy and effectiveness of the risk management, control and governance processes to support the SIC. The SIC is an extremely important statement that covers the whole of an organisation and is a board responsibility. Chief executives and boards will be held to account if they sign a statement that subsequent events show they did not understand or take seriously.

Detailed guidance on SICs is available on the Department of Health's website.

In FTs the annual governance statement fulfils the same function as the SIC.

The role of executive directors and staff

The first line of assurance to any board or stakeholder consists of the organisation's executive directors and line managers and in particular their personal integrity and work standards. The systems and processes that they are responsible for are also critical in assurance terms.

The role of auditors, regulators and inspection agencies

In terms of providing independent assurance, auditors, regulators and inspection agencies play a vital role. Indeed, experience suggests that the higher the risk area, the more value independent assurance provides. At the same time it is important to remember that these organisations have their own statutory responsibilities.

The remainder of this chapter focuses on those organisations and functions that are of particular importance in relation to risk management and assurance. You may also want to refer back to chapter 4 which looks at the roles played by a number of key external organisations.

External audit

The public is entitled to expect that money raised by local or national taxation is well used and accounted for properly. In this respect, external audit is an important source of assurance to the board and stakeholders. Chapter 4 explains the two key roles of the external auditor in the NHS, namely to report on:

- the annual accounts
- arrangements for securing economy, efficiency and effectiveness in the use of resources.

The Department of Health's 2003 guide *Delivering Excellence in Financial Governance* makes the point that the external auditor is a 'valuable source of advice on interpretation of central guidance and directives' and that 'the development of constructive working relationships ... and early discussion of areas of actual or potential concern can be invaluable in learning how to deal with them'. Close cooperation will also help the auditors to produce high quality and relevant outputs that can reinforce the assurance framework.

Internal audit

Internal audit is defined in the *NHS Internal Audit Standards* as 'an independent and objective assurance and consulting activity designed to add value and improve an organisation's operations. It helps an organisation accomplish its objectives by bringing a systematic, disciplined approach to evaluate and improve the effectiveness of risk management, control and governance processes'.

Under the current regime, all NHS bodies are required to have an internal audit service and the Head of Internal Audit's opinion is a key element of the framework of assurance that the accountable officer needs to inform the annual SIC.

As the definition above indicates, an internal audit service has two key functions – assurance and consultancy. The first of these is to provide an independent and objective opinion to the accountable officer, board and audit committee on the extent to which risk management, control and governance arrangements support the aims of the organisation.

'Risk management, control and governance' means the policies, procedures and operations established to ensure:

- the achievement of objectives
- the appropriate assessment of risk
- the reliability of internal and external reporting and accountability processes
- compliance with applicable laws and regulations
- compliance with the behavioural and ethical standards set for the organisation.

For example, in relation to auditing risk management processes, *NHS Internal Audit Standards* states that in 'determining whether risk management processes are effective is a judgement resulting from the internal auditor's assessment that:

- organisational objectives support and align with the organisation's mission
- significant risks are identified and assessed
- appropriate risk responses are selected that align risks with the organisation's risk appetite
- relevant risk information is captured and communicated in a timely manner across the organisation, enabling staff, management and the board to carry out their responsibilities
- risk management processes are monitored through ongoing management activities, separate evaluations, or both'.

The second function of internal audit is to provide an independent and objective consultancy service specifically to help line management improve the organisation's risk management, control and governance. When performing consulting services, the internal auditor must maintain objectivity and not take on management responsibility.

In practice this means that boards and managers can look to internal audit to:

- review the adequacy and effectiveness of internal control
- independently comment on risk identification

- bring key risks to the attention of senior management through their reports
- highlight areas of concern to the audit committee/board
- carry out reviews/investigations
- liaise with external auditors/other regulators
- provide assurance to management/audit committee/board that controls are operating effectively.

Internal audit can therefore offer an independent, ongoing review of the adequacy and effectiveness of the organisation's control environment – provided it is has sufficient resources and is well directed (the *NHS Audit Committee Handbook* indicates how directors can satisfy themselves on the effectiveness of their internal audit service).

Guidance is also available form the Internal Audit Practitioners' Group (IAPG) – a national grouping of internal audit practitioners that meets to inform overall policy and produce guidance for all internal auditors in the NHS.

NHS Protect

In April 2011, NHS Protect was established to 'undertake those anti crime functions that cannot be delivered at a local level across the NHS in England'.[3] This includes the work of the former Counter Fraud Service (CFS) which had responsibility for all policy and operational matters relating to the prevention, detection and investigation of fraud and corruption in the NHS.

NHS Protect is part of the NHS Business Services Authority and 'leads on a wide range of work to protect NHS staff and resources from crime. It has national responsibility for tackling:

- fraud
- violence
- bribery
- corruption
- criminal damage
- theft
- other unlawful action such as market-fixing'.

Under the NHS Protect approach, every health body will continue to nominate a suitable, trained officer to be its local counter fraud specialist (LCFS), who will act as the 'first line of defence' against fraud and corruption, in accordance with Secretary of State's Directions. All staff engaged in counter fraud work must be trained and accredited by NHS Protect. Although FTs are not bound by these directions they have LCFSs through the terms of their healthcare contracts.

Further guidance is provided in *Countering Fraud in the NHS* and *A Professional Approach to Managing Security in the NHS* – both published in 2003.

---

[3] NHS Protect Performance Report 10/11.

There is also a Treasury/National Audit Office guide that focuses on 'external fraud' – in other words, fraud that involves third parties (for example, businesses, individuals or organised crime groups) stealing money either by obtaining payments to which they are not entitled or keeping monies they should pay over to the Department. This guide – *Good Practice in Tackling External Fraud* – is available from the NAO's website.

Key questions for the organisation to consider

1. How does our organisation demonstrate accountability?
2. Is the board clear about what it has delegated and to whom?
3. Do we understand what an assurance framework is for and how it is developed?
4. Are we involved in developing, reviewing and maintaining the assurance framework and is it used to focus board discussions?
5. Is the assurance framework clear and understandable?
6. Do we understand the principal objectives in the assurance framework? Do we recognise them and was the board involved in establishing them?
7. Have the principal risks been explained to the board? Do we understand the controls which are expected to mitigate these?
8. Do we understand the sources of assurance? What evidence do we have that these sources are reliable and sufficient?
9. Do we know how to differentiate between the value and relevance of sources of assurance?
10. Do we know what to do when we receive 'negative' assurances?
11. What assurance does the board have that emerging priorities are brought to their attention?
12. Is everyone familiar with the organisation's system of internal control? Are we as an organisation able to assess whether or not gaps in control identified in the assurance framework cast doubt on the effectiveness of the overall system?
13. Is the board asked to approve the action plans to address gaps in control and gaps in assurance? Does it receive clear and regular progress reports on these action plans?
14. How is the board informed of progress on actions planned to address issues brought to its attention?
15. What assurance does the board have that these are followed through to an effective outcome?
16. Does the board receive exception reports on items still outstanding?
17. Has the concept of 'risk appetite' been discussed by the board? Has the board been involved in agreeing the organisation's risk appetite?
18. Has the board agreed escalation procedures for risks? Are relevant staff aware of these procedures and are they followed?
19. Does the organisation have a clear and comprehensive risk management strategy? What evidence do we have that it covers all activities and objectives?
20. Is the process for populating the organisation's risk register clear? How are the principal risks identified? Do we understand how the principal risks link to the assurance framework?

21. Are the controls and processes described in the organisation's SIC familiar to board members? Does the chief executive provide the board with a full briefing on the system of internal control?
22. Does the board receive summary reports on the results of internal audit work? Is this work well directed? Does it lead to effective remedial actions or change of practice where necessary?
23. Are routine performance reports produced for all activities (not just for finance)? Are these clear and understood by their intended audience, especially by NEDs? Is the information behind them reliable? How do we know?
24. How does the board know that the information it receives is reliable?
25. Does the board receive summary reports of the work of the LCFS?
26. How does the board know that items reported to it are the important ones?
27. Do we have procedures for 'escalating' risks that are above the agreed risk appetite?

This chapter's main learning points

- The chief executive is responsible for maintaining a sound system of internal control
- All NHS organisations are required to make an annual statement on internal control, which includes a requirement to maintain an assurance framework
- Each organisation must design their own assurance framework based on an understanding of the significant risks to its principal objectives
- Every organisation in the NHS must have a risk management strategy that underpins the system of internal control and plays a key role in the assurance framework
- It is not enough to identify risks and put them in a risk register: risk management is an active and continuous process that is concerned with opportunities as well as threats
- Good risk management requires leadership and commitment from the top and ownership throughout the organisation
- Every organisation should assess its risk appetite
- Every organisation should have in place procedures for escalating risks that exceed the risk appetite
- Auditors (internal and external), regulators and inspection agencies play a vital role in giving independent assurance and are a valuable source of advice and guidance
- All NHS bodies must have an internal audit service
- Fraud and corruption can occur in any organisation and it is important that the assurance framework includes measures to safeguard against it
- Every health organisation has a local counter fraud specialist.

Further reading

Taking it on Trust: A review of how NHS trusts and foundation trusts get their assurance, Audit Commission, 2009:
www.audit-commission.gov.uk/nationalstudies/health/financialmanagement/Pages/takingitontrust29april2009.aspx

The NHS Audit Committee Handbook, HFMA 2011:
www.hfma.org.uk/publications-and-guidance/

Building the Assurance Framework: a Practical Guide for NHS Boards, Department of Health, 2003:
www.dh.gov.uk/en/Publicationsandstatistics/Publications/PublicationsPolicyAndGuidance/DH_4093992

Corporate Governance in Banks and Other Financial Industry Entities (the Walker review), 2009:
www.hm-treasury.gov.uk/d/walker_review_261109.pdf

Alarm National Performance Model for Risk Management in the Public Services:
www.alarm-uk.org/publications.aspx

IIA Position Statement on Risk Based Internal Auditing, 2003:
www.iia.org.uk/en/index.cfm

NHS Operating Frameworks, Department of Health:
www.dh.gov.uk/en/Publicationsandstatistics/Publications/PublicationsPolicyAndGuidance/DH_122738

Internal Control: Guidance for Directors on the Combined Code (The Turnbull Report), 1999:
www.icaew.com/en/library/subject-gateways/corporate-governance/codes-and-reports

Delivering Excellence in Financial Governance, Department of Health, 2003:
www.dh.gov.uk/en/Publicationsandstatistics/Publications/PublicationsPolicyAndGuidance/DH_4006437

NHS Internal Audit Standards, Department of Health:
www.dh.gov.uk/en/Publicationsandstatistics/Lettersandcirculars/Dearcolleagueletters/DH_4110071

NHS Protect website:
www.nhsbsa.nhs.uk/Protect.aspx

NHS Protect Performance Report 10/11: www.nhsbsa.nhs.uk/Documents/CounterFraud/PERFORMANCE_REPORT.pdf

Countering Fraud in the NHS, 2003:
www.nhsbsa.nhs.uk/CounterFraud/Documents/countering_fraud_nhs.pdf

A Professional Approach to Managing Security in the NHS, 2003:
www.nhsbsa.nhs.uk/Documents/sms_strategy.pdf

Good Practice in Tackling External Fraud, National Audit Office, 2008:
www.nao.org.uk/guidance_and_good_practice/good_practice/fraud_and_corruption.aspx

Chapter 8: Clinical Governance

Introduction

Earlier chapters of this guide have referred to the risks involved if governance is viewed as a series of separate strands covering clinical, financial or organisational aspects. One of the most significant consequences of this approach is that boards challenge more effectively those areas that they feel more comfortable with and which are easier to measure. For example, finance issues tended to receive greater attention than the quality of healthcare. As governance is to do with how an organisation is structured and run across **all** its activities, this approach can lead to difficulties, particularly if boards lose sight of the fact that the overriding priority of the NHS is to improve the quality of healthcare.

The danger of an insufficient focus on clinical governance issues or an 'un-integrated' approach to governance generally has been all too evident in recent years in each of the high profile clinical failures referred to earlier in this guide including Maidstone and Tunbridge Wells NHS Trust, Mid-Staffordshire NHS Foundation Trust, Bristol Royal Infirmary, Alder Hey and Shipman. It is also implicitly recognised by the Chief Medical Officer (CMO) who has said, 'When I express concern about the priority given to the quality of safety of care by NHS managers and boards compared to financial balance and productivity targets, I am told not to worry because performance is judged on a 'balanced scorecard'. I sometimes feel that the reality is more like a 'scratch card' where the money and service activity boxes are revealed but quality and patient safety remained covered over'.[1]

This chapter aims to explain why clinical governance is such an important element of integrated governance and how it should best operate in an organisation.

What is clinical governance?

Clinical governance, like any other aspect of integrated governance is concerned with openness, integrity and accountability. The concept of clinical governance was first described in the 1997 white paper, *The new NHS: modern, dependable*. The most commonly used definition is 'a framework through which NHS organisations are accountable for continuously improving the quality of their services and safeguarding high standards of care, by creating an environment in which clinical excellence will flourish'.[2]

In other words, clinical governance is about putting in place the right people, policies and processes to deliver high quality healthcare. It is also to do with how NHS organisations:

- quality assure their services
- ensure those services are safe
- go about continually improving quality.

---

[1] Sir Liam Donaldson, speaking at The Health Foundation European Quality Meeting at Danesfield House Hotel, Marlow-on-Thames, Buckinghamshire on Saturday, 26 November 2005.
[2] G Scally and L J Donaldson, Clinical governance and the drive for quality improvement in the new NHS in England, BMJ, July 1998.

Clinical governance is also concerned with holding:

- clinicians to account for their decisions
- organisations to account for creating the conditions in which health professionals can deliver quality care.

Good clinical governance involves:

- identifying and managing risk
- quickly detecting and investigating adverse events and learning lessons from them in a blame free way
- developing a questioning and learning culture
- disseminating good practice
- having systems in place to ensure continuous improvements in clinical care
- high calibre leadership from the chief executive, medical director and nursing director (or equivalents) and clinicians in the front line delivering care to patients.

In practice this means that clinical governance embraces:

- quality – for example, effective treatment; services that are quick, easy to use and well organised
- the patient's experience – for example, how patients feel about the way they are treated and what would make things better? Are their preferences respected? Is there sufficient information and support?
- safety – for example, avoiding unintended harm whilst patients are being treated
- culture – for example, attitudes towards patients; relationships between clinicians and managers. Clinical governance depends on a culture that encourages openness and participation both among clinicians and between clinicians and non-clinicians (for example, managers and patients)
- organisational structures and policies – for example, are lessons learned and shared? Are there organisation wide policies that are known and understood? Is the organisation proactive rather than reactive?

Statutory requirements

The 1999 Health Act introduced a statutory 'duty of quality' on all health organisations. In practice this duty is fulfilled through an effective approach to clinical governance – in the words of the CMO, clinical governance is the 'local manifestation' of the duty of quality. This is further emphasised in *Clinical Governance: Quality in the New NHS*[3] which makes clear that the successful development and delivery of clinical governance is 'crucial to the overall success of the [quality] agenda'. As we have seen earlier in this guide, the emphasis on quality of care has become even more pronounced over recent years with:

---

[3] Department of Health circular 1999/065.

- *High Quality Care for all: NHS Next Stage Review Final Report* setting out a vision of an NHS that 'gives patients and the public more information and choice, works in partnership and has quality of care at its heart'
- the introduction via the *Health and Social Care Act 2008* of a registration process for all providers of health and adult social care services which have to demonstrate to the Care Quality Commission that they meet essential standards of quality and safety. The guidance that has been issued on compliance with these standards focuses on people and outcomes much more than policies and systems. This is consistent with the overall aim to improve the quality of care by putting the patient at the centre of NHS care through patient and public engagement
- the introduction from 2010 of quality accounts
- the Quality Board's 2011 report *Quality Governance in the NHS: a guide for provider boards* which made it clear that the 'primary focus of all NHS funded care is to be the delivering of improving quality and outcomes'.

Under the coalition government's planned changes to the NHS, clinical commissioning groups will take over PCTs' statutory duty to secure continuous improvement in the quality of services for patients. This will involve commissioning groups arranging for the provision of services that 'aim to secure improvements in physical and mental health, or in the prevention, diagnosis and treatment of illness'.[4] This will be achieved and measured through the *Commissioning Outcomes Framework* based on a number of quality standards for particular service areas. Both the reduction of inequalities in healthcare and the achievement of continuous improvement through effective commissioning will be rewarded through financial incentives and a quality premium, although the details of how this will work are not yet clear.

Structures for clinical governance

The board carries ultimate responsibility for clinical governance and is also required to ensure that there are 'appropriate structures' in place to oversee its operation. As there is no specific statutory requirement for a dedicated clinical governance committee, it is for each organisation to decide what best suits their local circumstances – the key issue being the need to have effective decision making forums. This means getting the right balance between those issues that the board discusses and takes responsibility for and those items that are delegated to a separate committee or committees.

Whatever structure is chosen, it is important to remember that boards cannot absolve themselves of responsibility for, or involvement with, clinical governance even if a dedicated committee exists.

Ensuring that clinical governance is effective

The detailed guidance that accompanied circular 1999/065 *Clinical Governance in the NHS* gave a few pointers that are helpful when assessing an organisation's approach. This says that 'for

---

[4] *The Functions of GP Commissioning Consortia, Department of Health*, March 2011: www.dh.gov.uk/prod_consum_dh/groups/dh_digitalassets/documents/digitalasset/dh_125006.pdf

clinical governance to be successful, all health organisations must demonstrate:

- an open and participative culture in which education, research and the sharing of good practice are valued and expected
- a commitment to quality that is shared by staff and managers, and supported by clearly identified local resources, both human and financial
- a tradition of active working with patients, users, carers and the public
- an ethos of multi disciplinary teams working at all levels in the organisation
- regular board level discussion of all major quality issues for the organisation and strong leadership from the top
- good use of information to plan and to assess progress.'

The Department's 2002 guidance *Clinical Governance Reporting Processes* set out in detail the issues that should be considered by trust boards and chief executives when reporting on clinical governance. Five areas were specified:

- the patient's experience – for example, planning and organisation of care; the environment of care, user involvement via patient advice and liaison services (PALS)
- use of information – for example, relating to the patient's experience; resources, processes and outcomes
- quality improvement processes – for example, risk management; clinical audit programmes; evidence based practice; learning from incidents and complaints
- staff – for example staffing and staff management; education, training and continuing professional development; multi disciplinary working
- leadership, strategy and planning – for example, community and patient involvement; organisation and clinical leadership; planning services and organisational performance review.

In 2005, the Clinical Governance Support Team (CGST) and the Appointments Commission published *Board Assurance Prompts* (BAPs) which set out questions boards might ask to assure themselves that governance arrangements are successfully supporting the organisation's strategic objectives. Although the CGST was wound up in 2008, the BAPs remain relevant – particularly with today's renewed focus on quality of care, the involvement of patients and use of information.

The headings under which these questions were presented are shown below:

Board assurance prompts developed by the Appointments Commission/Clinical Governance Support Team, 2005

1. Reduce serious adverse events within a given speciality
2. Control hospital and surgery acquired infections
3. Recruit and retain the right staff in the right roles
4. Manage staff vacancies within the trust
5. Ensure our financial and business planning will follow our strategic priorities
6. Ensure the trust is financially viable

7. Reduce costs by working differently
8. Develop our information systems to make informed decisions
9. Make aligned and coherent decisions
10. Ensure we have access to a wide range of views
11. Ensure professionals see the relevance of the information we ask them to collect
12. Ensure our care environments are fit for purpose
13. Ensure our range of care environments is appropriate
14. Ensure patients are fully involved in their progress along care pathways
15. Give patients the right range of choices
16. Ensure our services match the local health needs
17. Be a good corporate neighbour
18. Play our part in protecting health locally
19. Commission for sustainable quality
20. Reduce waiting times for surgery to a six monthly period
21. Follow recognised guidance and guidelines
22. Make information available on what we provide and to what standard.

One issue that is emphasised again and again when talking about clinical governance is the fact that it is not only for clinicians – rather it concerns both clinical and non-clinical staff, and acknowledges everyone's contribution to the patient's experience. This was re-iterated in the Quality Board's 2011 report which stated that 'the distinction between quality governance and clinical governance is less relevant as clinicians and managers are working towards the same ends – the delivery of the highest quality services.'

Clinical governance and medical professionals

In the first decade of the 21st century, new contracts for hospital consultants, GPs and other medical professionals formalised a requirement for regular appraisal. Clinical governance and appraisal came together in February 2007, with the Department of Health's publication *Trust Assurance and Safety*, which proposed reforms to professional regulation, including:

- measures to make regulators more independent, such as the appointment of council members, professional members no longer forming the majority of these councils and an independent adjudicator for doctors
- measures to ensure healthcare professionals are objectively revalidated throughout their career and remain up to date with clinical best practice
- the creation of GMC affiliates to help deal with more cases concerning doctors at a local level and to ensure independent oversight of aspects of revalidation
- changing the standard of proof used in fitness to practise cases from the criminal standard to the civil standard with a sliding scale
- moving towards a more rehabilitative approach to regulation, with the development of a comprehensive strategy for prevention, treatment and rehabilitation services for all health professionals.

On the same day, the government published its response to the Shipman inquiry, which included the following changes:

- better support for patients who want to register concerns and measures to ensure they are taken seriously
- making more systematic use of information about the clinical outcomes of individual practitioners and teams
- ensuring that information from different sources is brought together so that a fuller picture about professionals is properly considered
- requiring all primary care organisations to adopt best practice in investigating and acting on concerns.

Taken together these two documents aimed to:

- make the protection of patients and the public the first priority of all who are concerned with healthcare
- set out proposals which would sustain and enhance the high regard in which the public hold health professionals
- ensure that good regulation does not get in the way of good patient care.

Clinical governance and patients

The emphasis on quality of care is becoming increasingly associated with the aim of putting patients at the heart of NHS care. In May 2009 the Department of Health published *A Guide to Using Patient Feedback to Transform Services,* making clear once again the integrated nature of governance. Patient involvement is not just about patients' perceptions of the service they receive but an integral part of clinical planning, feedback and monitoring. The launch of this publication made it clear that patients' feedback on their experience of treatment and care is an important dimension of quality that should be used to drive change. The guide contains an annex with questions for board members to consider in relation to patient involvement – as shown below:

Understanding what matters: a guide to using patient feedback to transform services – annex B: questions for board members

Vision and culture

- what is the organisation's vision for improving patient experience?
- what is the organisation's strategy for communications and stakeholder engagement on patient experience issues?

Systems and processes

- does the organisation have clear ways of communicating with the public and local population in order to gauge their experience and expectations?
- over what timescale is the organisation planning to meet the *NHS Operating Framework* requirement and Secretary of State's commitment to using real-time patient experience feedback?
- does the organisation have clear systems in place to assess if a culture of improvement has taken root?

- does the board receive regular updates demonstrating the use of patient experience feedback?
- how will you feedback the results and actions to your patients and local population?

Responsibilities, capability and capacity

- is there a named board member with responsibility for improving patient experience?
- who is responsible for measuring patient experience?
- which senior clinical leaders are supporting the patient experience feedback programme?
- are they also committed to making quality improvements as a result of the programme?
- do staff have the right skills and do they have support from directors?

Patient involvement is also an overriding aspect of the CQC's *Essential Standards of Quality and Safety,* where many of the questions focus on what information patients are given and when; what questions they are asked and when; what matters they are consulted on and how their responses are dealt with. Using these tools, organisations can assess whether they are putting patients at the heart of care in practice and effectively.

The 2010 Francis Report on Mid-Staffordshire NHS Foundation Trust revealed that patients had suffered from multiple failures in management and governance and made some specific recommendations which are fundamental to effective governance in the NHS and apply beyond this particular trust – they are:

Francis report recommendations in relation to openness, quality of care and use of information

- The Trust, in conjunction with the Royal Colleges, the Deanery and the nursing school at Staffordshire University, should review its training programmes for all staff to ensure that high-quality professional training and development is provided at all levels and that high-quality service is recognised and valued.
- The board should institute a programme of improving the arrangements for audit in all clinical departments and make participation in audit processes in accordance with contemporary standards of practice a requirement for all relevant staff. The board should review audit processes and outcomes on a regular basis.
- The board should review the Trust's arrangements for the management of complaints and incident reporting in the light of the findings of this report and ensure that it:
  - provides responses and resolutions to complaints which satisfy complainants
  - ensures that staff are engaged in the process from the investigation of a complaint or an incident to the implementation of any lessons to be learned
  - minimises the risk of deficiencies exposed by the problems recurring
  - makes available full information on the matters reported, and the action to resolve deficiencies, to the board, the governors and the public.

- Trust policies, procedures and practice regarding professional oversight and discipline should be reviewed in the light of the principles described in this report.
- The board should give priority to ensuring that any member of staff who raises an honestly held concern about the standard or safety of the provision of services to patients is supported and protected from any adverse consequences, and should foster a culture of openness and insight.
- In the light of the findings of this report, the Secretary of State and Monitor should review the arrangements for the training, appointment, support and accountability of executive and non-executive directors of NHS trusts and NHS foundation trusts, with a view to creating and enforcing uniform professional standards for such posts by means of standards formulated and overseen by an independent body given powers of disciplinary sanction.
- The board should review the management and leadership of the nursing staff to ensure that the principles described are complied with.
- The board should review the management structure to ensure that clinical staff and their views are fully represented at all levels of the Trust and that they are aware of concerns raised by clinicians on matters relating to the standard and safety of the service provided to patients.
- The Trust should review its record-keeping procedures in consultation with the clinical and nursing staff and regularly audit the standards of performance.
- All wards admitting elderly, acutely ill patients in significant numbers should have multidisciplinary meetings, with consultant medical input, on a weekly basis. The level of specialist elderly care medical input should also be reviewed, and all nursing staff (including healthcare assistants) should have training in the diagnosis and management of acute confusion.
- All NHS trusts and foundation trusts responsible for the provision of hospital services should review their standards, governance and performance in the light of this report.

Independent Inquiry into care provided by Mid Staffordshire NHS Foundation, Robert Francis QC, February 2010.

Regulation and control

There are a number of organisations with a particular interest in the clinical governance arena which are discussed in turn below.

Care Quality Commission

From a regulatory perspective, the Care Quality Commission has a particular interest in clinical quality and governance and is responsible for operating a registration scheme for all providers of healthcare in England to ensure that they are meeting essential common quality standards. Its focus is on making sure that health and social care is 'high quality' which the CQC defines as 'care that:

- is safe

- has the right outcomes, including clinical outcomes (for example do people get the right treatment and are they well cared for?)
- is a good experience for the people who use it, their carers and their families
- helps to prevent illness, and promotes healthy, independent living
- is available to those who need it when they need it; and
- provides good value for money.'

The registration process requires NHS organisations to make a declaration of compliance with its essential standards of quality and safety. There are 28 essential standards but the CQC's judgement framework has a particular focus on the 16 essential standards and associated outcomes that most directly relate to the quality and safety of care experienced by people using a service – these are:

- care and welfare of people who use services
- assessing and monitoring the quality of service provision
- safeguarding vulnerable people who use services
- cleanliness and infection control
- management of medicines
- meeting nutritional needs
- safety and suitability of premises
- safety, availability and suitability of equipment
- respecting and involving people who use services
- consent to care and treatment
- complaints management
- records management
- requirements relating to workers
- staffing
- supporting workers
- cooperating with other providers.

The emphasis on patient safety is of particular importance and the responsibility of NHS boards in this area is unequivocal. As the CQC's website puts it: 'patients expect and are entitled to the safest possible care and the boards of NHS trusts are ultimately responsible for the safety of the care that their services provide.'

To help boards discharge their responsibilities, the CQC has published two reports that focus on improving the safety of care within the NHS:

- *Safe in the Knowledge* aims to help boards 'identify and develop the key behaviours, systems, and measures of improvement that they should review on a regular basis to determine whether they are truly commissioning and delivering the safest possible care, and if not, what needs to change'
- *Safely does it* sets out guidance designed to help drive improvement in the governance and implementation of safer care.

See chapter 4 for more about the CQC's responsibilities and regulatory approach.

NHS Litigation Authority

Although it is not a regulatory body, the NHSLA operates the clinical negligence scheme for trusts (CNST) and publishes a set of risk management standards for each type of healthcare organisation covering organisational, clinical, and health and safety risks. For example, for acute NHS trusts, PCTs and independent sector providers in 2011/12 there are detailed standards for:

- governance
- a competent and capable workforce
- a safe environment
- clinical care
- learning from experience.

Members of CNST are assessed against these standards to establish their risk rating within the scheme. For example, the 2011/12 'clinical care' risk standard looks at 10 separate criteria:

- patient information
- health record-keeping standards
- screening procedures
- diagnostic testing procedures
- medicines management
- transfusion
- resuscitation
- venous thromboembolism
- transfer of patients
- discharge of patients.

Ethics committees

There are currently around 190 NHS research ethics committees (RECs) in the UK which are responsible for 'providing independent advice on the extent to which proposals for research studies to be carried out within the NHS comply with recognised ethical standards'.[5] Their primary purpose when considering study proposals is to 'safeguard the rights, safety, dignity and well-being of people participating in research in the NHS.' They do this by reviewing research applications and giving an opinion about the proposed participant involvement and whether the research is ethical.

Clinical audit

The National Institute of Health and Clinical Excellence (NICE) and the Healthcare Quality Improvement Partnership (HQIP) define clinical audit as 'a quality improvement process that seeks to improve patient care and outcomes through systematic review of care against explicit criteria and the implementation of change'.

---

[5] Report of the Ad Hoc Advisory Group on the Operation of NHS Research Ethics Committees, Department of Health, June 2005.

In its guide – *Best Practice in Clinical Audit* – NICE states that it sees clinical audit as being 'the component of clinical governance that offers the greatest potential to assess the quality of care routinely provided for NHS users' and that it (clinical audit) 'should therefore be at the very heart of clinical governance systems'. The Audit Commission also recognised the critical role that clinical audit plays in its 2009 guide *Taking it on Trust* where clinical audit is described as 'the review of clinical performance, the measurement of performance against agreed standards and the refining of clinical practice as a result'. As such, 'it is one of the key compliance tools at management's disposal and has an important role within the assurance agenda'.

Clinical audit is a process that is carried out by healthcare professionals themselves and involves:

- setting standards
- measuring current practice
- comparing results with standards
- changing the way things are done
- re-auditing to make sure practice has improved.

For NHS boards, managing clinical risk is of equal, or greater, importance than managing financial and business risk and good clinical audit is an enormous asset and source of assurance. In addition, organisations are required to declare their participation in clinical audit in the annual quality accounts.

In its guide *Clinical Audit: a simple guide for NHS Boards and Partners* HQIP set out twelve criteria for good local clinical audit:

1. Clinical audit should be part of a structured programme.
2. Topics chosen should in the main be high risk; high volume or high cost or reflect national clinical audits, national service frameworks or NICE guidance.
3. Service users should be part of the clinical audit process.
4. Should be multidisciplinary in nature.
5. Clinical audit should include assessment of process and outcome of care.
6. Standards should be derived from good quality guidelines.
7. The sample size chosen should be adequate to produce credible results.
8. Managers should be actively involved in clinical audit and in particular in the development of action plans from clinical audit enquiry.
9. Action plans should address the local barriers to change and identify those responsible for service improvement.
10. Re-audit should be applied to ascertain whether improvements in care have been implemented as a result of clinical audit.
11. Systems, structures and specific mechanisms should be made available to monitor service improvements once the clinical audit cycle has been completed.
12. Each clinical audit should have a local lead.

Since April 2010 the NHSLA risk management standards have included a standard on clinical audit, which aims to establish that each organisation has a formal process for ensuring that all clinical audit work is undertaken, completed and reported on in a systematic way that is implemented and monitored. For more details see the NHSLA's website.

Council for Healthcare Regulatory Excellence

The CHRE was set up following the Kennedy Report into events at Bristol Royal Infirmary in April 2003 by the *National Health Service Reform and Health Care Professions Act 2002*. Its mission is to 'protect the public interest, promote best practice and achieve excellence in relation to regulating healthcare professionals ... and to contribute to developing professionally-led regulation in healthcare to protect the public'. The CHRE covers all of the UK and 'promotes best practice and consistency in the regulation of healthcare professionals by the following nine regulatory bodies:

- General Chiropractic Council
- General Dental Council
- General Medical Council
- General Optical Council
- General Osteopathic Council
- Health Professions Council
- Nursing and Midwifery Council
- Pharmaceutical Society of Northern Ireland
- Royal Pharmaceutical Society of Great Britain.

The CHRE is funded by the Department of Health and reports to the UK Parliament. Although the CHRE's area of interest is in monitoring how regulators of healthcare professionals are functioning, its website will be of interest to NHS bodies. Also of relevance is the 2008 publication *Implementing the White Paper Trust, Assurance and Safety: enhancing confidence in healthcare professional regulators – final report and Department of Health response to recommendations.*

Following a review soon after it came to power, the coalition government plans to retain the CHRE but not as an Arm's Length Body – instead it will become self-funding through a levy on the bodies it regulates.

Key questions for the organisation to consider

1. Is our organisation fulfilling its duty of quality? How do we know?
2. Do our organisation's governance principles and practices apply equally to the management of clinical activities?
3. Does the organisation's assurance framework include strategic clinical objectives and the risks, controls and assurances relating to these?
4. What evidence do we see that good clinical risk management is applied in our organisation?
5. Does the board receive regular reports on the quality of clinical care and outcomes? Is the board involved in setting policy and monitoring performance in relation to quality of care?

6. Do we produce regular reports on patients' experience and patients' involvement (for example, how patients feel about the way they are treated and what would make things better? Are their preferences respected? Is there sufficient information and support?)

7. Are these reports considered by the board? Is the board involved in setting policy and monitoring performance in relation to both increasing patient involvement and measuring and improving patients' experience?

8. What evidence do we have that there is openness in dealing with clinical incidents? Are lessons learnt from clinical incidents? Are these lessons shared with other disciplines? Are there organisation wide policies that are known and understood? Is the organisation proactive rather than reactive?

9. Are summary reports of complaints and clinical negligence claims prepared and considered by the board? Do we identify common themes arising from these? How do these reports correlate to other risks/performance issues?

10. Is there a culture of openness between clinicians and management throughout the organisation?

11. Does the organisation refer to the CQC's guidance when developing and reviewing its approach to clinical governance?

12. How do we ensure that we meet the NHSLA's clinical care and clinical audit standards?

13. How is the clinical audit plan developed? Does it cover the right areas of clinical risk/clinical objectives? Does the board receive summary reports of the nature and results of clinical audit work? Is this work well directed? Does it lead to remedial actions or change of practice where necessary?

14. Does our organisation review regularly the clinical audit function and ensure that it is performing as it should?

15. Do we monitor and review the results of national inquiries into clinical failings in other organisations? What evidence is provided of our organisation's status relative to the findings of these inquiries? Are appropriate actions to prevent similar occurrences decided and implemented?

This chapter's main learning points

- The overriding objective of NHS organisations is to deliver high quality healthcare – this is not possible without effective clinical governance
- Clinical governance is concerned with how NHS bodies quality assure their services, make sure those services are safe and improve their quality
- All health organisations have a statutory duty of quality which is fulfilled through effective clinical governance
- The board is responsible for clinical governance as part of the wider integrated governance agenda and must ensure that appropriate structures are in place
- The board cannot absolve itself of responsibility for clinical governance even if a dedicated committee has been set up
- When reporting on clinical governance, boards need to consider the patient's experience, the use of information, quality improvement and processes and staff

- The Care Quality Commission looks at the level of quality that healthcare bodies (including FTs, private and voluntary providers of care) achieve
- The NHSLA has standards on clinical care and clinical audit
- Ethics committees are responsible for 'safeguarding the rights, dignity and welfare of people participating in research in the NHS'
- Clinical audit is particularly important to the management of clinical risk and improving quality of care
- The CHRE exists to 'protect the public interest, promote best practice and achieve excellence in relation to regulating healthcare professionals…and to contribute to developing professionally-led regulation in healthcare to protect the public'.

Further reading

The New NHS: modern, dependable, Department of Health, 1997:
www.archive.official-documents.co.uk/document/doh/newnhs/forward.htm

Clinical governance and the drive for quality improvement in the new NHS in England, BMJ 1998:
www.bmj.com/content/317/7150/61.full

High Quality Care for all: NHS Next Stage Review Final Report, Department of Health, 2008:
www.dh.gov.uk/en/Publicationsandstatistics/Publications/PublicationsPolicyAndGuidance/DH_085825

Quality Governance in the NHS: a guide for provider boards, Department of Health, 2011:
www.dh.gov.uk/en/Publicationsandstatistics/Publications/PublicationsPolicyAndGuidance/DH_125238

Department of Health circular 1999/065 Clinical Governance in the NHS:
www.dh.gov.uk/en/Publicationsandstatistics/Lettersandcirculars/Healthservicecirculars/DH_4004883

The Functions of GP Commissioning Consortia, Department of Health, 2011:
www.dh.gov.uk/en/Publicationsandstatistics/Publications/PublicationsPolicyAndGuidance/DH_124979

Trust Assurance and Safety: the Regulation of Health Professionals, Department of Health, 2007:
www.dh.gov.uk/en/Publicationsandstatistics/Publications/PublicationsPolicyAndGuidance/DH_065946

The Shipman Inquiry: www.the-shipman-inquiry.org.uk/

A Guide to Using Patient Feedback to Transform Services, Department of Health, 2009:
www.dh.gov.uk/en/Publicationsandstatistics/Publications/PublicationsPolicyAndGuidance/DH_099780

Essential Standards of Quality and Safety, CQC:
www.cqc.org.uk/usingcareservices/essentialstandardsofqualityandsafety.cfm

Robert Francis Inquiry Report into Mid-Staffordshire NHS FT, 2010:
www.dh.gov.uk/en/Publicationsandstatistics/Publications/PublicationsPolicyAndGuidance/DH_113018

Safe in the Knowledge, CQC, 2009:
www.cqc.org.uk/_db/_documents/Safe_in_the_knowledge_200903273451.pdf

Safely does it, CQC, 2009:
www.cqc.org.uk/_db/_documents/Safely_does_it_200903274336.pdf

NHSLA: www.nhsla.com/home.htm

Risk Management Standards – CNST: www.nhsla.com/riskmanagement

Report of the Ad-hoc Advisory Group on the operation of NHS Research Ethics Committee, Department of Health, 2005:
www.dh.gov.uk/en/Publicationsandstatistics/Publications/PublicationsPolicyAndGuidance/DH_4112416

Best Practice in Clinical Audit – NICE:
www.nice.org.uk/media/796/23/BestPracticeClinicalAudit.pdf

Taking it on Trust: A Review of how Boards of NHS Trusts and NHS Foundation Trusts get their Assurance, Audit Commission, 2009:
www.audit-commission.gov.uk

Clinical Audit: a Simple Guide for NHS Boards and Partners, HQIP, 2010:
www.hqip.org.uk/assets/Guidance/HQIP-Simple-Guide-LEAFLET.pdf

Inquiry into the Management of Care of Children Receiving Complex Heart Surgery at the Bristol Royal Infirmary:
www.bristol-inquiry.org.uk

National Health Service Reform and Healthcare Professions Act 2002:
www.legislation.gov.uk/ukpga/2002/17/contents

Implementing the White Paper Trust, Assurance and Safety: enhancing confidence in healthcare professional regulators – final report and Department of Health response to recommendations, Department of Health, 2008:
www.dh.gov.uk/prod_consum_dh/groups/dh_digitalassets/@dh/@en/documents/digitalasset/dh_085161.pdf

Chapter 9: Governance in NHS Foundation Trusts

Introduction

NHS foundation trusts (FTs) were created as new legal entities in the form of public benefit corporations by the *Health and Social Care (Community Health and Standards) Act 2003* – now consolidated in the *NHS Act 2006*. The Act sets out the minimum legislative requirements for the governance of FTs but within this framework FTs can tailor their governance arrangements to suit the individual circumstances of their community and health economy, reflecting the range of diverse relationships with patients, the local community and other stakeholders.

FTs remain part of the NHS with the primary purpose of providing NHS services to NHS patients according to NHS principles and standards. In particular, the public continues to receive free care, based on need not ability to pay. However, FTs have greater freedom to innovate and are released from direct government control. Instead they are accountable to Parliament via the Independent Regulator, Monitor (see chapter 4).

FTs possess four key characteristics that distinguish them from NHS trusts:

- freedom to decide locally how to meet their obligations
- accountability to local people, who can become FT members and governors
- authorisation and regulation by Monitor
- a duty to engage with local communities and encourage local people to become members of the organisation. This duty is central to the public benefit (or mutual) model on which the constitution of FTs is based.

The coalition government's expectation is that by 2014 all remaining non foundation NHS trusts will achieve foundation status although this is not a 'blanket deadline'.

Becoming a foundation trust

To qualify for authorisation to operate as an FT, applicants must meet stringent criteria set by the Department of Health and pass Monitor's rigorous assessment process.

Before an NHS trust can apply to Monitor to become an FT it must first work with its SHA to develop a 'robust and credible' FT application in what is referred to as the development phase. This involves (inter alia) a public consultation process of at least 12 weeks and the development of an integrated business plan and long term financial model. When the SHA is satisfied that the trust is ready to proceed, a formal application is made to the Secretary of State. This is known as the 'Secretary of State support phase' and involves an applications committee that considers the trust's application and advises the Secretary of State on whether or not the trust should be supported to proceed to Monitor's assessment phase.

Monitor's assessment phase takes approximately three months and focuses on three key criteria:

- is the trust well governed?

- is the trust financially viable?
- is the trust legally constituted?

The process also involves a 'board to board meeting' which is held midway through the assessment period and is designed to allow the applicant board to 'demonstrate that it is aware of the risks facing the trust and provide details on how these risks can or have been managed and mitigated. It also provides Monitor's board with a key opportunity to question the non-executive directors of the trust to determine whether they have the skills required to effectively challenge the executive team.'[1]

Applicants meeting the required standards are granted a licence that establishes them as an FT in the legal form of a public benefit entity and Monitor issues its terms of authorisation which sets out the conditions under which the FT must operate (see below).

Constitution and authorisation

In preparing for foundation status, trusts must demonstrate that they are legally constituted. The main components of the constitution are:

- the eligibility criteria for membership and the designation of membership constituencies
- the composition and operating arrangements of the board of directors and the board of governors – including the role of the chair
- provisions for the conduct of governor elections
- details of the circumstances when a governor or director may be disqualified or removed
- provisions for dealing with conflicts of interest
- details of the FT's 'registers' (for its members, governors and directors. For governors and directors the registers must include their interests)
- standing orders for both the board of directors and the board of governors
- details about the appointment of the auditor
- the purpose of the audit committee
- the preparation and adoption of the annual financial plan and accounts.

The requirements placed on FTs are set out in their terms of authorisation, issued by Monitor once they have been granted FT status. In particular, FTs are required by their authorisation to:

- put and keep in place, maintain and comply with arrangements for the purpose of improving the quality of healthcare provided by and for that trust
- deliver healthcare services to specified standards under legally binding contracts with their commissioners
- maintain registration with the Care Quality Commission and address conditions associated with registration
- operate effectively, efficiently and economically and as a going concern
- comply with healthcare targets and indicators

---

[1] Monitor's website – *Becoming an NHS Foundation Trust.*

- govern themselves in accordance with best practice, maintaining the organisation's capacity to deliver mandatory services
- grow a representative membership
- cooperate with the Care Quality Commission and a range of NHS and non-NHS bodies which may have a remit in relation to the provision of healthcare services
- disclose information to Monitor and third parties according to the detailed requirements set out in their authorisation
- deal openly and cooperatively with Monitor, including regarding potential or actual breaches of compliance with their authorisation or any serious reputational issues
- comply with statutory requirements, their authorisation, their constitution, their contracts with commissioners and guidance issued by Monitor
- follow the *Principles and Rules of Cooperation and Competition* and take such action as may be required by Monitor, advised by the Cooperation and Competition Panel, to address a breach of the *Principles and Rules of Cooperation and Competition*
- have regard to the *NHS Constitution*.

In meeting the requirements of their authorisation, FTs must decide for themselves how best to organise and manage themselves so as to optimise effectiveness, efficiency and economy of service delivery. FTs are managed by their board of directors who are accountable to members via the board of governors.

Monitor expects boards to report any risks that could materially affect compliance.

Under the coalition government's planned reforms, the role of Monitor will expand to become the economic regulator and from 2016 it will no longer be responsible for overseeing FTs.

Making the most of being a public benefit corporation

The constitution of a public benefit corporation draws on the traditions of mutual organisations established under Industrial and Provident legislation. In practice this means that each FT has a membership from which a board of governors is elected. The FT has a duty to consult and involve the board of governors, comprising patients, staff, members of the public and other key stakeholders, in the strategic planning of the organisation. Governors are then accountable to the members of the FT– patients, carers, staff and members of the public – from whom they are elected. By acting as a two-way conduit, the board of governors facilitates the direct incorporation of local influence in setting the overall direction of the FT alongside regularly feeding back information from the FT to its members. These governance structures enable FTs to actively engage their stakeholders in shaping plans to make health services more responsive to the needs of individual patients and the health needs of the communities they serve.

By strengthening connections between hospitals and their local communities, this form of public ownership and accountability is designed to ensure that hospital services more accurately reflect local needs and expectations. However, the public continue to receive healthcare according to core NHS principles – free care, based on need and not ability to pay. The thinking behind this approach is that as public benefit corporations, FTs are better able to improve care for their patients by being set free from central government control. Although they must still operate to national healthcare standards and targets, they are not performance managed through strategic health authorities and are free to determine their own strategic direction.

From a financial perspective, FTs are not required to break even each year and may retain any operating surpluses to invest in the delivery of new services. They are able to decide locally the investment needed in order to improve their services and increase their capacity and are able to borrow to support this investment, without needing to seek external approval. However they must comply with rules and regulations set by Monitor including its *Prudential Borrowing Code*. This protects the public and patients by ensuring that the FT does not take on more debt than it can manage. An FT must remain within a prudential borrowing limit (PBL) set by Monitor based on its ability to repay any loans it enters into. The PBL is the **maximum** amount of debt which the FT can have outstanding at any point in time and is specified in the terms of its authorisation. It is reviewed at least annually in conjunction with the annual plan, and variations can be made upwards or downwards.

To ensure that NHS patients do not lose out as a result of the introduction of FTs, there are provisions in the originating Act, which place a 'lock' on the purpose of any FT. Of these, two safeguards or restrictions stand out:

- **existing non-current assets**: any proposed change in the use (including sale) of scheduled or protected non-current assets must be authorised by Monitor. Protected assets are identified at the time of application in terms of the protected services delivered from them. When granting a license to an FT, Monitor will take due regard of the protected assets for subsequent monitoring. Moreover, protected assets cannot be pledged as security for loans
- **private patient income cap**: to ensure that the estate and future growth in services of an FT benefit NHS patients, the Act places a cap on the growth in private patient activity. Specifically, the Act requires that the proportion of income from private activity as a proportion of total income must be no greater than it was for the predecessor NHS trust. In other words if private income was 3% of defined income in 2002/03 (in most circumstances the 'base financial year'), then it must not exceed 3% of defined income in 2003/04 and beyond.

  Following a challenge by UNISON, the public sector trade union, which culminated in judicial review at the High Court in December 2009 Monitor revised its rules and guidance in relation to private patient income to make clear that 'income receivable by an FT as an entity which is derived from and has its origins in private patient activity is what is important, irrespective as to whether that activity is delivered directly by the FT or indirectly through another entity'.

  For mental health FTs, the cap on private income was amended by the *Health Act 2009* so that it is now the proportion of total income derived from such charges in 2002/03 (which for many trusts was 0%) or 1.5% if greater.

  Under the coalition government's proposals, FTs will have their private patient cap removed but will need to produce separate accounts for NHS and private-funded services.

Membership and elections

Organisations preparing for foundation status must devise a membership strategy, which defines the membership community and appropriate constituencies, from which governors are to be elected. Members vote to elect governors and can also stand for election themselves.

FTs have a duty to engage with local communities and encourage local people to become members of the organisation. This duty is central to the mutual model on which the constitution of FTs is based.

Legislation states that FTs must take steps to ensure that the membership is representative of the communities they serve. Eligibility criteria for membership vary between FTs depending on their local circumstances. As a minimum, membership of an FT will be open to:

- people who live in the local area
- staff
- if an FT's constitution provides for it, people who live outside that area but have been patients or carers of patients treated at one of the FT's hospitals; and people who exercise functions for the FT but who are not employed by the organisation (for example, staff employed in a PFI venture).

While FTs are required to have two constituencies (for the public and for staff), they are free to decide whether to have a constituency for patients.

All FTs are required to establish registers of members, directors and governors. These registers must, as a minimum, contain a list of names and, in the case of directors, state their interests.

'Model election rules' were published by the Department of Health to assist applicant trusts in drafting their constitution. The model rules include a proposed minimum timetable for the key stages in the election process, and the requirement that there must be independent scrutiny of the elections as overseen by a returning officer.

The board of directors should monitor how representative the FT's membership is and the level and effectiveness of member engagement. This information should then be used to review the FT's membership strategy and inform the board statements accompanying the annual plan submission.

The role of the board of governors

Unlike other NHS organisations, the FT structure includes governors to represent local interests and to 'bind a trust to its patients, service users and stakeholders'.[2] These governors consist of both elected and appointed individuals who represent FT members and other stakeholder groups (including the public, patients and staff). When applying to be a member of the FT, an individual applicant can also confirm an interest in becoming a governor.

---

[2] *Your Statutory Duties: a Reference Guide for NHS Foundation Trust Governors*, Monitor, 2009.

Legislation provides for each FT to decide on the size and shape of its board of governors in the light of their local circumstances, within certain minimum parameters set out in legislation:

- more than half of the members of the board of governors must be elected from the public and, where applicable, patient membership
- there must be at least three staff governors elected from the staff membership, or where there are classes within the staff constituency at least one governor from each class
- there must be at least one local authority governor, one PCT governor and (where applicable) at least one university governor, all via nomination.

Over and above these minimum requirements there can be as many other governors as an individual FT sees fit provided there are more public governors than all the other governors put together. However, Monitor's *Code of Governance* does emphasise that 'the board of governors should not be so large as to be unwieldy' and recommends that its role, structure, composition and procedures be reviewed regularly.

It is a legal requirement that the chair of the FT is both the chair of the board of governors and the board of directors. This ensures that views from governors are considered by the directors and gives the chair a pivotal role in the organisation.

The main function of the board of governors is to advise the FT on how it carries out its work so that it is consistent with the needs of its members and wider community. It does this by working closely with the board of directors to ensure that the FT acts in a way that is consistent with its terms of authorisation and to help set the strategic direction.

The board of governors is also responsible for appointing the FT's chair and non-executive directors (NEDs) and the external auditors. In addition, the board of directors must obtain the approval of the board of governors before they can appoint a chief executive officer.

The lead governor

The board of governors can nominate a lead governor with a specific role to:

- facilitate communications between the governors and the board of directors
- be involved with setting the agenda for board of governor meetings to ensure that the concerns of governors are included
- chair the board of governor meetings when constitutionally appropriate (for example, if the meeting is discussing the appointment or removal of the chair or the deputy)
- contribute to the appraisal of the chair by the nominations committee
- act as a point of contact with Monitor through the governors instead of through the FT (this route would only be used in exceptional circumstances – for example, if the board of governors has serious concerns that the FT is at risk of significantly breaching its terms of authorisation and the concerns have not been resolved).

The lead governor role does not have either statutory or constitutional powers but facilitates the smooth operation of the board of governors.

Working with a board of governors

Monitor's *Code of Governance* states that the board of governors is responsible for representing the interests of the members and partner organisations in the local health economy in the governance of the FT. Governors are expected to act in the best interests of the FT and 'to hold the board of directors to account for the performance of the trust including ensuring the board of directors acts so that the FT does not breach its terms of authorisation'. There are a variety of ways in which this can happen and may include the following:

- holding discussions with pathfinder clinical commissioning groups
- challenging hospital performance in relation to quality indicators
- raising specific concerns following staff survey results
- reviewing, shaping and challenging the future strategy of the FT including the annual financial plan
- developing options for reinvesting any surpluses ensuring that patients' needs and views are taken into account
- setting up working groups/sub committees to prepare reports for the board of directors on specific issues.

The board of governors is also responsible for sharing information about key decisions with their membership community. This may be through themed public meetings held in the council wards or through working with local GP patient groups.

Monitor's *Code of Governance* gives more details about the role of governors and emphasises that they 'must act in the best interests of the FT and should adhere to its values and code of conduct'. It also states that 'the roles and responsibilities of the board of governors should be set out in a written document'.

The role of the board of directors

Every FT must have an effective board of directors that consists of executive directors (which must include the chief executive and finance director) and NEDs. The chair of the board must be a NED. NEDs should have particular experience or skills that help the board function well. They are appointed by the board of governors based on recommendations made by a nominations committee.

Monitor's *Code of Governance* emphasises that the board of directors is 'collectively responsible' for every decision it takes regardless of individual directors' skills or status. In particular, the board of directors must set the FT's strategic aims (taking account of the views of the board of governors) and is responsible for 'ensuring compliance by the FT with its terms of authorisation, its constitution, mandatory guidance issued by Monitor, relevant statutory requirements and contractual obligations'.

The board of directors is also responsible for:

---

[3] *The NHS Foundation Trust Code of Governance*, Monitor.

- providing leadership of the FT within a framework of internal control which enables risk to be managed effectively
- reviewing management performance
- ensuring the quality and safety of healthcare services, education, training and research delivered by the FT and applying the principles and standards of clinical governance set out by the Department of Health, the Care Quality Commission, and other relevant NHS bodies
- setting the FT's values and standards of conduct and ensuring that its obligations to its members, patients and other stakeholders are understood and met.

The role of NEDs on the board of directors is different from their traditional role in NHS trusts. This is due in part to representation of local communities on the board of governors. As members of a unitary board, NEDs must take equal responsibility and accountability for the functioning and success of the business. They also have a duty to ensure appropriate challenge is made – particularly in relation to the FT's executive management.

Accountability and audit

The *Code of Governance* states that the board of directors 'should present a balanced and understandable assessment of the FT's position and prospects'. This responsibility extends to 'all public statements and reports to regulators and inspectors, as well as information required to be presented by statutory requirements'. The board of directors is also responsible for 'maintaining a sound system of internal control to safeguard public and private investment, the FT's assets, patient safety and service quality'.

The board of directors is also charged with notifying Monitor and the board of governors 'without delay' of 'all relevant information which is not public knowledge concerning a material change:

- in the FT's financial condition
- in the performance of its business
- in the FT's expectations as to its performance which, if made public, would be likely to lead to a substantial change to the financial wellbeing, healthcare delivery performance or reputation and standing of the FT.'

The board must establish an audit committee composed of at least three independent NEDs and at least one member needs to have recent and relevant financial experience.

The main role and responsibilities of the audit committee are similar to those of NHS trusts, with the additional requirement to make recommendations to the board of governors in relation to the appointment, re-appointment and removal of the external auditor and to approve the remuneration and terms of engagement of the external auditor.

The *Audit Code for NHS Foundation Trusts,* published by Monitor, prescribes the way in which external auditors are to carry out their functions.

As with other NHS organisations, FTs must have an 'accounting officer' (the chief executive) who 'is responsible to Parliament for the resources under their control' Monitor has issued its own accounting officer memorandum which sets out the responsibilities in detail. Similarly, finance directors of FTs are automatically executive directors with a seat on the board – as in other NHS trusts. Chapter 5 gives further information about the role of accounting (or 'accountable') officers and finance directors.

The audited annual accounts must be laid before Parliament and the chief executive, as accounting officer, may be required to appear before the Public Accounts Committee to answer questions. See chapter 6 for more about annual accounts.

Relationship with Monitor

At present, Monitor is responsible for authorising, monitoring and regulating FTs and assesses risk and intervenes to ensure compliance with all aspects of the authorisation. To monitor the performance of FTs, Monitor has established a risk-based compliance framework which it reviews (and consults on) each year. This means that assessments of risk in a number of key areas are used to determine the level and depth of monitoring that an FT is subject to. From 2010/11 Monitor focuses on two areas – finance and governance (including mandatory services).

To make its assessment in both areas, Monitor relies primarily on the information it receives directly from FTs (including annual plans and in-year monitoring submissions), but it also considers third party reports on a variety of specific issues, in particular those of other regulatory bodies. Details of Monitor's *Compliance Framework*, its approach to risk ratings and FTs' current scores are available on its website.

Finance risk rating

A financial scorecard is used to generate a finance risk rating (FRR). It looks at five ratios within four criteria – for each criterion a score of one to five is awarded with one indicating a high risk of a significant breach of the terms of authorisation and five a low risk with no financial regulatory concerns.

An FT is rated in each of these metrics and then, using weightings, an overall aggregate FRR is produced. This is a whole number from one to five, where 1 indicates a high risk of financial instability and 5 a low risk.

Governance risk rating

The governance risk rating focuses on the degree to which FTs are complying with their terms of authorisation. Monitor looks at five criteria here:

- service performance
- third party views in relation to the Care Quality Commission (CQC) and the NHS Litigation Authority (NHSLA)
- provision of mandatory services
- other certification failures where boards have failed to accurately self-certify and the failure is material
- other factors (which can include failure to meet the statutory requirements of other bodies).

A scoring system is used to assess governance risk levels and a graduated 'traffic light' rating (green; amber-green; amber-red; red) is linked to those scores. For example, if an FT achieves a green rating it indicates that there are 'no material concerns' (i.e. a low risk) whilst a red rating signifies that there is 'likely or actual significant breach of authorisation' (i.e. a high risk). The scores and their related traffic light ratings are refreshed each year in Monitor's *Compliance Framework*.

The scoring system also takes into consideration the need for all healthcare providers to comply with the registration requirements of the CQC. If the CQC attaches conditions to an FT's registration, the governance risk rating is adversely affected.

The relationship of FTs with Monitor is based on effective self-governance, and the board of directors takes primary responsibility for compliance with the authorisation. The chair has a key role in ensuring that the board of directors monitors the performance of the FT in an effective way and satisfies itself that action is taken to remedy problems as they arise. The board must complete a number of self-certified statements alongside submission of the annual plan as well as during the year, confirming that the FT has the appropriate arrangements in place to meet all requirements in relation to:

- quality
- mandatory services
- service performance
- risk management processes
- the terms of its authorisation
- roles, structures and capacity (including the capacity and capability of the board of directors and the adequacy of the management structure).

FTs must initially report on a quarterly basis to ensure that they comply with their authorisation. Because the compliance regime is risk-based, well-governed high-performing trusts are given space to exercise their freedoms and may be required to report only at six-monthly intervals. However, where FTs are experiencing major financial or service problems, oversight is more intensive and monthly reporting may be required.

Monitor also has extensive powers to intervene in the event that an FT is failing to comply with its authorisation. In particular, section 52 of the *NHS Act 2006* allows Monitor to:

- 'require the FT to do, or not to do, specific things within a set period
- remove any or all of the directors or members of the board of governors and appoint interim directors or members of the board of governors.'

The *Health Act 2009* sets out two ways in which an FT can be de-authorised:

- failure to comply with a notice issued under section 52 and Monitor is satisfied that the FT is unable to provide the goods and services required under its authorisation (this is allowed for under section 65D of the 2009 Act)
- failing to comply with its authorisation and Monitor 'is satisfied that that the seriousness of the failure justifies de-authorisation' (this is allowed for under section 52B of the 2009 Act).

At present, de-authorisation means that an FT becomes an NHS trust. However, this will change once the *Health and Social Care Bill 2011* is enacted and any de-authorised FT will be merged with one or more existing FTs. If this is as a result of invoking section 65D a trust special administrator will also be appointed. For full details of the intervention regime, refer to Monitor's *Compliance Framework*.

Monitor has recognised the importance of effective governance in the success of every FT and has published the *NHS Foundation Trust Code of Governance* to promote the key principles of good governance and how to apply them. This best practice code is based very closely on the private sector *Combined Code* (now the *UK Corporate Governance Code*) and is not mandatory. However, the code does impose disclosure requirements on FTs – namely to report on how the main and supporting principles in the code are applied and either to confirm compliance or explain non compliance.

Key questions for the organisation to consider

1. Are we all aware of (and do we understand) our terms of authorisation?
2. Do we meet all the disclosure requirements set out in our terms of authorisation?
3. Do we engage with local communities to encourage membership? Is our membership representative? Do we review regularly our strategy in this area?
4. Do we regularly review our membership categories – for example to consider whether or not we need a patient constituency?
5. Are the respective roles and responsibilities of the board of governors and board of directors clear and understood by all?
6. Do members of both boards (and all staff) understand the relationship between the board of directors and the board of governors?
7. Is the communication between the board of directors and board of governors effective? If not, what needs to be done to improve things?
8. Is the role of the lead governor clear and understood?
9. Is everyone clear about the roles and responsibilities of the accounting officer?
10. Are our processes for self certification returns to Monitor robust?
11. How does the board obtain the assurances necessary to enable the self certification returns to be signed with confidence?
12. Are we confident of the process to appoint and remove the external auditor including the role of the audit committee and the board of governors?
13. Do we regularly review our conduct in relation to the FT Code of Governance?

This chapter's main learning points

- FTs are public benefit corporations. They are free from central government control, accountable to local people and regulated by Monitor
- NHS trusts wishing to achieve foundation status must meet strict criteria set by the Department of Health and undergo rigorous assessment processes established by Monitor

- FTs are free to act within the terms of their authorisation
- As legally constituted public benefit corporations, FTs are able to design their services to meet the needs of their local communities
- FTs have a duty to engage with local communities, to encourage local people to become members of the organisation and to ensure that the membership is representative of the communities they serve
- The board of directors takes primary responsibility for compliance with its authorisation
- NEDs take equal responsibility and accountability for the functioning and success of the business
- The board of governors represents the interests of local people and partner organisations in the governance and operations of the FT and in advising on the trust's strategic direction
- The board of directors must notify Monitor and the board of governors of any significant issues, not in the public domain, which may affect the financial position, healthcare delivery performance or reputation and standing of the FT
- The lead governor must notify Monitor if significant concerns raised by the board of governors fail to be resolved satisfactorily
- Monitor has established a risk-based compliance framework for the purpose of monitoring the performance of FTs and has extensive powers of intervention in the event of an FT failing to comply with its authorisation
- Monitor issues a Code of Governance setting out best practice guidance.

Further reading

Health and Social Care (Community Health and Standards) Act 2003:
www.legislation.hmso.gov.uk/acts/acts2003/20030043.htm

Monitor website:
www.monitor-nhsft.gov.uk/home/our-publications

Of particular relevance are the following Monitor publications:

NHS Foundation Trust Code of Governance

NHS Foundation Trust Model/Core Constitution

Compliance Framework

Prudential Borrowing Code

Audit Code for NHS Foundation Trusts

Revised Terms of Authorisation for NHS Foundation Trusts

NHS Foundation Trust Accounting Officer Memorandum

Your Statutory Duties: a Reference Guide for NHS Foundation Trust Governors

Principles and Rules of Cooperation and Competition, Department of Health, 2010:
www.dh.gov.uk/en/Publicationsandstatistics/Publications/PublicationsPolicyAndGuidance/DH_113746

UNISON Judicial Review: www.unison.org.uk/asppresspack/pressrelease_view.asp?id=1673

Health Act 2009: www.legislation.gov.uk/ukpga/2009/21/contents

Model Election Rules (part of the constitution), Monitor:
www.monitor-nhsft.gov.uk/home/our-publications/browse-category/guidance-applicants/model-core-constitution

NHS Act 2006: www.legislation.gov.uk/ukpga/2006/41/contents

UK Corporate Governance Code, 2010: www.frc.org.uk/corporate/

Chapter 10: Governance in Northern Ireland

Chapters 1 and 2: What is Governance?/How the Elements of Governance fit together

The key concepts of governance as outlined in chapters 1 and 2 of this guide are equally relevant to health and social care (HSC) organisations in Northern Ireland. This chapter highlights key differences to indicate how these concepts have been taken forward in Northern Ireland.

Corporate governance in the NHS/HSC

The principles of governance are common to HSC organisations in Northern Ireland and many of the directives and circulars are similar.

In Northern Ireland the *Codes of Conduct and Accountability* were distributed in the form of circular HSS (PDD) 8/94 in November 1994. New editions, revised in light of the recent reforms in public administration in Northern Ireland, will be published shortly. *A Code of Practice on Openness* was published by the HPSS in December 1996.

There have been many other circulars issued providing guidance on aspects of governance – a full list is available from the Department of Health, Social Services and Public Safety's (DHSSPS) website: www.dhsspsni.gov.uk/governance-guidance

One circular that remains worthy of particular note is DAO (DFP) 18/2005 which introduced HM Treasury's *Code of Good Practice in Central Government Departments*.

This Code was approved by ministers and is intended to clarify how departmental management boards function, as well as their relationship to ministers and accounting officers. It also provides guidance on the relationship between departments and their arm's length bodies.

The Code itself does not apply to HSC bodies, but it does contain guidance on best practice in a number of areas. All HSC bodies are enjoined to follow the Code's precepts, and all have incorporated them, to an appropriate degree, in their ways of working.

Controls assurance

The controls assurance regime that was introduced by the Department of Health during the 1990s has been withdrawn in England but continues to operate and develop in Northern Ireland.

Circular HSS (PPM) 5/2003 advised that when a controls assurance standard is issued formally, HSSPS bodies are expected to conduct an initial self-assessment against the key criteria and draw up an action plan to secure compliance.

For 2011/12, twenty two standards are in place. Compliance with the three 'core' standards:

- financial management
- governance
- risk management

is regarded as fundamental in underpinning individual Statements of Internal Control (SICs) and providing the basis for compliance with the remaining standards; all organisations must comply with them. In addition, there are nineteen non-core standards where compliance depends on relevance to an organisation's particular business:

- buildings, land, plant and non-medical equipment
- decontamination of medical devices
- emergency planning
- environmental cleanliness
- environmental management
- fire safety
- fleet and transport management
- health and safety
- human resources
- infection control
- information and communications technology
- management of purchasing and supply
- medical devices and equipment management
- medicines management
- records management
- waste management
- research governance
- food hygiene
- security management.

Chapter 3: Public Sector Values and Organisational Culture

In November 2003 the DHSSPS issued Circular HSS (SM) 4/2003: *Code of Conduct for HPSS Managers* to chief executives of all HPSS (now HSC) bodies, for immediate implementation.

The Code sets out the core standards of conduct expected of managers. It serves two purposes:

- to guide HSC managers and employers in the work that they do and the decisions and choices they have to make
- to reassure the public that these important decisions are being made against a background of professional standards and accountability.

This Code sets out certain important contractual obligations that apply to everyone holding management positions. This includes chief executives, directors and senior managers who as part of their duties are personally accountable for achieving high quality care. Employers should also identify other managers who should comply with the Code because of their level of responsibility and accountability.

For all posts at chief executive, director and senior manager level employers are required to:

- include the Code in new employment contracts
- incorporate the Code into the employment contracts of existing staff at the earliest practicable opportunity.

Alongside this Code, HSC managers must also follow:

- the Nolan Principles
- *Codes of Conduct and Accountability* (circular HSS (PDD) 8/94, issued in November 2004)
- guidance on the provision of hospitality (issued under HSS (F) 8/2003 in April 2003)
- *Standards of Business Conduct for HPSS staff* (HSS (GEN 1) 1/95, March 1995)
- the *Code of Practice on Openness in the HPSS*
- standards of good employment practice.

Chapter 4: The External Regulatory Framework

The role of Government

The Northern Ireland Assembly was established in 1999 as part of the Belfast Agreement and consists of 108 members, 6 from each of the 18 constituencies.

A First Minister and Deputy First Minister are appointed from among the members and head an executive committee of ministers. Ministers are nominated by their party in accordance with the proportion of seats obtained at an Assembly election. The Secretary of State for Northern Ireland remains responsible for Northern Ireland Office matters that are not devolved to the Assembly. These include:

- international relations
- taxation
- national insurance
- regulation of financial services
- regulation of telecommunications and broadcasting.

The Secretary of State represents Northern Ireland's interests in the United Kingdom Cabinet.

Role of the Department of Health, Social Services and Public Safety (DHSSPS)

Health and social care in Northern Ireland are the responsibility of the Minister for Health, Social Services and Public Safety. The Department of Health, Social Services and Public Safety (DHSSPS) was established by the *Departments (NI) Order 1999* and is the largest of all Northern Ireland Departments. In 2011/12 the Department's budget was £4.4bn, some 42% of the total NI Executive DEL revenue budget. Of this £3.7bn was budgeted for health and social care (including family health services).

The DHSSPS's current remit covers policy and legislation relating to:

- health and social care (this includes hospitals, family practitioner services, community health and social services)
- public health (to promote and protect the health and wellbeing of the population of Northern Ireland)
- public safety (this includes the Fire and Rescue Service, food safety and emergency planning).

The Department's mission statement is to improve the health and social wellbeing of the people of Northern Ireland. It endeavours to do so by:

- leading a major programme of cross-government action to improve the health and wellbeing of the population and reduce health inequalities. This includes interventions involving health promotion and education to encourage people to adopt activities, behaviours and attitudes which lead to better health and wellbeing. The aim is a population which is much more engaged in ensuring its own health and wellbeing
- ensuring the provision of appropriate health and social care services, both in clinical settings such as hospitals and GPs' surgeries, and in the community through nursing, social work and other professional services.

The Permanent Secretary of the Department is also Chief Executive of the Health and Social Care system, as well as accounting officer for all the Department's responsibilities.

Within the Department, the key business groups are the Resources and Performance Management Group, the Healthcare Policy Group the Health Estates Investment Group (HEIG), the Office of the Chief Medical Officer and the Office of Social Services.

There are five professional groups within the department, each led by a Chief Professional Officer:

- Medical and Allied Services
- Social Services Inspectorate
- Nursing and Midwifery Advisory Group
- Dental Services
- Pharmaceutical Advice and Services.

Health and Social Care Board

The Health and Social Care Board (HSCB) is accountable to the Minister for translating his vision for health and social care into a range of services that deliver high quality and safe outcomes for users, good value for the taxpayer and compliance with statutory obligations. This includes ensuring that commissioning is effective (and to that end commissioning plans are developed in close partnership with the Public Health Agency), performance management and service improvement, and resource management.

A full description of the responsibilities of the HSCB can be accessed from their website at www.hscboard.hscni.net/

HSC trusts

There are six HSC trusts in Northern Ireland, five of them area-based (Belfast, Northern, South Eastern, Southern and Western) offering a range of acute and community services. The sixth Trust, the Northern Ireland Ambulance Service, operates the ambulance service for Northern Ireland. More information is available from individual Trust websites.

Other HSC organisations

A variety of specialist or support functions are carried out by organisations on a Northern Ireland-wide basis. These include:

- Public Health Agency
- Business Services Organisation
- Northern Ireland Blood Transfusion Service
- Northern Ireland Guardian Ad Litem Agency
- Northern Ireland Practice and Education Council for Nursing and Midwifery
- Northern Ireland Medical and Dental Training Agency
- Northern Ireland Social Care Council
- Regulation and Quality Improvement Authority.

On the Department's website will be found a *Framework Document* which describes the roles and functions of the various health and social care bodies and the systems that govern their relationships with each other and the Department (see www.dhsspsni.gov.uk/framework_document_september_2011.pdf). In addition, information on all the organisations referred to above can be accessed from their websites (listed at the end of this chapter).

Local commissioning groups

There are five local commissioning groups (LCGs):

- Belfast
- Northern
- South Eastern
- Southern
- Western.

Each LCG is a committee of the HSCB and is co-terminus with its respective HSC trust area.

LCGs are responsible for the commissioning of health and social care by addressing the care needs of their local population. They also have responsibility for assessing health and social care needs; planning health and social care to meet current and emerging needs; and securing the delivery of health and social care to meet assessed needs.

Role of regulatory/inspection agencies

Northern Ireland Audit Office (NIAO)

The NIAO combines the roles of the Audit Commission and the National Audit Office. The Comptroller and Auditor General for Northern Ireland (C&AG) is the head of the NIAO. He is appointed by the Crown and has two main functions:

- authorisation of the issue of public funds to government departments and other public sector bodies
- the audit of central government finances.

The *Northern Ireland Act 1998* ensures that the C&AG is totally independent in the exercise of his functions.

The *Audit and Accountability (Northern Ireland) Order 2003* came into effect on 1 April 2003. This Order addresses the organisation of public sector audit in Northern Ireland and also audit and accountability issues raised by Lord Sharman of Redlynch's report *Holding to Account, the Review of Audit and Accountability for Central Government*, published in 2001.

The C&AG is required by statute to examine and certify the accounts of all Northern Ireland government departments and a wide range of other public sector bodies, including executive agencies, NDPBs and health and social care bodies. He also audits a number of central government accounts by agreement with the Department of Finance and Personnel and the bodies concerned and, on behalf of the National Audit Office, the accounts of the Northern Ireland Office and its associated bodies.

Financial audit work is conducted in accordance with international standards on auditing (UK & Ireland) and in compliance with the Auditing Practices Board's *Ethical Standards for Auditors*. The main object is to provide the Assembly with reasonable assurance that the financial statements (accounts) audited by the NIAO:

- give a true and fair view
- have been properly prepared in accordance Department of Finance and Personnel directions made under the *Government Resources and Accounts Act (NI) 2001*
- have applied in all material respects expenditure and income to the purposes intended by the Assembly and the financial transactions conform to the authorities that govern them.

In addition to reporting the results of this work to Parliament and to the Assembly, the NIAO also aims to provide client bodies with constructive advice that will help them improve their corporate governance, financial management, control and reporting.

The NIAO examines risks to regularity, propriety and the conduct of public business in central government bodies and reports on significant weaknesses to the Assembly. This work involves the exercise of the C&AG's rights to inspect public bodies where he is not the appointed auditor.

The C&AG has statutory authority to undertake VFM examinations in those bodies where he is the appointed auditor or has rights of access and inspection by statute or by agreement. The primary objectives of VFM audit are to:

- provide the Assembly/Parliament with independent information and advice about how economically, efficiently and effectively departments, agencies and other bodies have used their resources
- help audited bodies improve their performance in achieving VFM.

Duty of Quality

Under the *Health and Personal Social Services (Quality Improvement and Regulation) (Northern Ireland) Order 2003* a statutory duty of quality is imposed on HSC organisations. This means that each organisation, large or small, has a legal responsibility to ensure that the services it provides meet a required standard.

Delivery of health and social care services is increasingly complex and it is in the interests of commissioners, providers, service users and carers that there is an integrated and consistent approach to demonstrating quality in service delivery. The duty of quality is intended to create 'umbrella' or overarching standards that will sensibly incorporate the many standards that already exist. These broad high-level standards, known as 'themes' are applicable to any health and social care environment whether community, primary or tertiary care.

The five quality themes are:

- corporate leadership and accountability of organisations
- safe and effective care
- accessible, flexible and responsive services
- promoting, protecting and improving health and social wellbeing
- effective communication and information.

The Regulation and Quality Improvement Authority (RQIA)

The Regulation and Quality Improvement Authority is an independent body, established by the DHSSPS on 1 April 2005. It has overall responsibility for monitoring and inspecting the availability and quality of health and social care services in Northern Ireland and encouraging improvements in the quality of those services.

RQIA has two main functions. Firstly, it inspects the quality of health and social care services provided by HSC bodies in Northern Ireland. These inspections take the form of reviews of clinical and social care governance arrangements within these bodies.

Secondly, the Authority regulates (registers and inspects) a wide range of health and social care services delivered by HSC bodies and by the independent sector. The regulation of services is based on minimum care standards that ensure that service users know what quality of services they can expect to receive and service providers have a benchmark against which to measure the quality of their services. So far five sets of standards have been published:

- nursing homes
- residential care homes
- nursing agencies standards
- domiciliary care agencies
- residential family centres.

Further standards covering the range of health and social care services regulated under the *HPSS (Quality, Improvement and Regulation) (NI) Order 2003* will be published in due course.

Chapter 5: Organisational Structures: Running an NHS Organisation

The general principles of organisational structure as set out in chapter 5 are consistent with arrangements in Northern Ireland. This includes roles and responsibilities of boards, chief executives, board members (including non-executives), the audit committee and the remuneration committee. One difference to note is that all appointments to HSC organisations are made by the DHSSPS.

Regarding specific committees or individual roles, the situation for the HSC is outlined below:

Audit committee

Codes of Conduct and Accountability – HSS (PDD) 8/94 sets out the requirement for each organisation to establish an audit committee.

Local commissioning groups

The five LCGs are in several respects analogous to primary care trusts (PCTs) in England. LCGs, as committees of the HSC Board, have responsibility for assessing health and social care need in their respective areas, planning to meet those needs and securing the delivery of a comprehensive range of services to meet the needs of the local population. They bring together providers of local primary and community services under a management board whose membership is drawn from representatives of primary care professionals, the community and service users, as well as HSC boards and trusts.

Clinical and social care governance

In Northern Ireland, the term clinical governance is replaced by 'clinical and social care governance'. Comprehensive guidance is set out in *Governance in the HPSS Clinical and Social Care Governance: Guidelines for Implementation HSS (PPM) 10/2002*, issued in January 2003.

Risk management

Guidance on populating a risk register and risk management has been issued by the DHSSPS. A number of circulars have been issued on the subject, including:

- *Making it Happen: a Guide for Risk Managers on how to Populate a Risk Register* (October 2002)
- *Corporate Governance: Statement on Internal Control, HSS (PPM) 3/2002* (June 2002)
- *Risk Management in the Health and Personal Social Services, HSS (PPM) 8/2002* (October 2002)
- *Governance in the HPSS: Risk Management, HSS (PPM) 13/2002* (December 2002)
- *Governance in the HPSS: Risk Management and Controls Assurance, HSS (PPM) 5/2003* (April 2003)
- *AS/NZS 4360:2004 – Risk Management, HSS (PPM) 4/2005* (June 2005).

Chief executive/accounting officer

As noted in chapter 5, the chief executive is the accounting officer in respect of the total funds allocated to the organisation. In summary, accounting officers have personal responsibility for the propriety and regularity of the public finances in their organisations.

In Northern Ireland the line of accountability for the accounting officer is as follows:

Northern Ireland Assembly

↑

Minister for Health, Social Services and Public Safety

↑

DHSSPS permanent secretary (accounting officer)

↑

HSC body (accounting officer) – chief executive

Chapter 6: Internal Systems and Processes: Statutory Requirements

Accountability

In Northern Ireland the *Codes of Conduct and Accountability* are set out in HSS (PDD) 8/94.

Priorities and planning framework

The Minister's priorities for health and social care are set out in an annual *Commissioning Plan Direction*. The current Direction was issued in June 2011, following the Assembly elections in May.

Standing orders (SOs), standing financial instructions (SFIs), reservation and delegation of powers

The requirement and content for SOs, SFIs and a scheme of delegation as set out in chapter 6 is consistent with requirements within the HSC. HSS (F) 13/07, issued in March 2007, sets out a series of model documents covering various financial governance issues.

Performance monitoring

See comments on chapter 4 and *Governance in the HPSS – Clinical and Social Care Governance: Guidelines for Implementation HSS (PPM) 10/2002* issued in January 2003.

Annual reports and accounts

Requirements in Northern Ireland are covered by sections E and F of the *Codes of Conduct and Accountability HSS (PDD) 8/94* issued in November 1994. The annual report and accounts are prepared in accordance with the *Government Financial Reporting Manual* (FReM) as interpreted for the HSC through the annual accounts manual issued by the DHSSPS; and through various circulars.

Chapter 7: Risk Management and the Assurance Framework

Risk management

The contents of chapter 7 are consistent with the position in Northern Ireland. However, it was made clear in circular HSS (PPM) 8/2002 (issued in October 2002) that there are important structural, legislative and service differences between the NHS and HSC. For the latest guidance refer to: www.dhsspsni.gov.uk/hss/governance.

The Statement on Internal Control

Governance in the HPSS: Risk Management and Controls Assurance – HSS (PPM) 5/2003 issued in April 2003 set out the requirements in respect of statements on internal control (SICs) in Northern Ireland. The SIC is prepared in accordance with the FReM as interpreted for the HSC through the annual accounts manual issued by the DHSSPS; and supplemented by circulars as appropriate.

Clinical/medical negligence

In March 2010 HSC (SQSD) 05/10 *Handling clinical and social care negligence and personal injury claims* was issued, giving guidance to HSC organisations on the procedures that should be followed in the management of all negligence and other personal injury claims. Further guidance was issued in December 2010 through HSC (F) 58/2010 on the accounting arrangements.

External audit

The position is somewhat different in Northern Ireland and is summarised as follows.

The *Audit and Accountability (Northern Ireland) Order 2003* came into effect on 1 April 2003. This Order addresses the organisation of public sector audit in Northern Ireland and also audit and accountability issues raised by Lord Sharman of Redlynch's report *Holding to Account, The Review of Audit and Accountability for Central Government,* published in 2001. This widened the role of the Comptroller and Auditor General (C&AG) – see the comments on chapter 4 for details.

Counter fraud

In 2005 the Permanent Secretary of the DHSSPS issued a *Counter Fraud Strategy* for the Department and its associated bodies, introducing mandatory requirements for:

- fraud policy statement
- fraud response plan
- whistle blowing policy
- induction training
- fraud awareness training
- risk assessments.

Counter Fraud and Probity Services (CFPS)

CFPS was established within the Business Service Organisation in April 2009 – its remit includes:

- tackling fraudulent claims by patients to exemption from statutory dental and ophthalmic charges
- formal investigation of cases of potential or suspected fraud across all HSC organisations
- delivery of a range of probity, verification and assurance work in relation to primary care contractors
- counter fraud and probity policy issues.

A Fraud Hotline has been set up to enable both staff and the public to report suspicious incidents confidentially. The Hotline is an anonymous, free phone and confidential service open to members of the public, users of the service and staff. A protocol has been developed to ensure that all matters raised through the hotline are followed up in accordance with fraud investigation best practice.

Further information on the CFPS can be found on the Business Service Organisation's website: www.hscbusiness.hscni.net/index.htm

Chapter 8: Clinical Governance

The requirements regarding clinical governance in Northern Ireland are set out in comments on chapter 5. Quality improvement measures in Northern Ireland are covered in comments on chapter 4.

Chapter 9: Governance in NHS Foundation Trusts

There are no foundation trusts in Northern Ireland.

Further reading

Department of Health, Social Services and Public Safety: www.dhsspsni.gov.uk/

Health and Social Care Board: www.hscboard.hscni.net

Patient Client Council: www.patientclientcouncil.hscni.net

Belfast Health and Social Care Trust: www.belfasttrust.hscni.net

South Eastern Health and Social Care Trust: www.setrust.hscni.net

Southern Health and Social Care Trust: www.southerntrust.hscni.net

Northern Health and Social Care Trust: www.northerntrust.hscni.net

Western Health and Social Care Trust: www.westerntrust.hscni.net

Northern Ireland Ambulance Service: www.niamb.co.uk

Public Health Agency: www.publichealth.hscni.net

Business Services Organisation: www.hscbusiness.hscni.net

Regulation and Quality Improvement Authority: www.rqia.org.uk

Northern Ireland Guardian Ad Litem Agency: www.nigala.hscni.net

Northern Ireland Social Care Council: www.niscc.info

Northern Ireland Medical and Dental Training Agency: www.nimdta.gov.uk

Northern Ireland Practice and Education Council for Nursing and Midwifery: www.nipec.hscni.net

Northern Ireland Blood Transfusion Service: www.nibts.org

Review of Public Administration Implementation: www.rpani.gov.uk/

DHSSPS – review of public administration pages:
www.dhsspsni.gov.uk/index/hss/rpa-home.htm

DHSSPS website – governance pages (includes circulars):
www.dhsspsni.gov.uk/governance-guidance

Controls Assurance: www.dhsspsni.gov.uk/governance-controls

Northern Ireland Audit Office (NIAO): www.niauditoffice.gov.uk

Duty of Quality: www.dhsspsni.gov.uk/governance-quality

Chapter 11: Governance in NHSScotland

Chapters 1 and 2: What is Governance?/How the Elements of Governance fit together

The key concepts of corporate governance as outlined in chapters 1 and 2 of this guide are equally relevant to NHSScotland. This chapter highlights how these concepts have been taken forward in Scotland.

Chapter 3: Public Sector Values and Organisational Culture

One of the first Acts of the Scottish Parliament was the *Ethical Standards in Public Life etc. (Scotland) Act 2000*. This established the Standards Commission for Scotland, which enforces codes of conduct for councillors (approved by the Scottish Parliament) and those appointed to devolved public bodies (approved by Scottish Ministers). The Commission works with 32 local authorities and 129 other public bodies.

These Codes promote the Nolan principles, and essentially set out what the Scottish public expect of those elected or appointed to public office.

Another important early piece of legislation was the *Public Finance and Accountability Act (2000)*. This established Audit Scotland, the Auditor General, and the role of accountable officers, and set out the landscape of accountability for public expenditure.

Within Scottish health boards the board's chief executive is the accountable officer. The accountable officer is personally responsible for the propriety and regularity of public finances given to the board, and for ensuring that resources are used economically, efficiently, and effectively.

Within the detailed responsibilities of the accountable officer is a duty to ensure that arrangements have been made to secure best value. In March 2011, the Scottish Government issued revised guidance on best value which revisited previously published best value characteristics and identified the following specific themes:

- vision and leadership
- effective partnerships
- governance and accountability
- use of resources
- performance management.

The specific themes are supported by two cross-cutting themes – sustainability and equality.

The chief executive can be required to account for the performance of the duties of accountable officer to the Scottish Parliament's Public Audit Committee.

This revised guidance is intended to be used across all public bodies in Scotland, not just the NHS.

Since 2007, the Scottish Government has established a national performance framework, which sets out:

- the Government's purpose
- five strategic objectives
- fifteen national outcomes to be achieved in ten years
- 45 national indicators to track progress on the above.

Within Scotland there is a strong emphasis on partnership working between public bodies and their partners towards delivering against the national performance framework.

With respect to matters of personal conduct of NHS employees (who are not subject to the *Ethical Standards Act*), there are two extant publications:

- MEL (1994) 48 – *Standards of Business Conduct for NHS Staff*
- HDL (2003) 62 – *A Common Understanding: Guidance on Joint Working between NHSScotland and the Pharmaceutical Industry.*

A further aspect of values and organisational culture which must be recognised is the *Staff Governance Standard*. This was developed as a result of *The National Health Service (Scotland) Reform Act* of 2004 which introduced a duty on every health board and special health board in relation to the governance of staff.

The *Staff Governance Standard* focuses on five key principles to ensure that staff are:

- appropriately trained
- provided with a safe working environment
- well informed
- involved in decisions which affect them, and
- treated fairly and consistently.

Compliance with the Standard is subject to monitoring by the local partnership forum, through a national staff survey and the completion of a self-assessment audit tool.

Chapter 4: The External Regulatory Framework

Role of Government

The Scottish Government is the executive arm of the devolved government for Scotland.

The Scottish Government, known as the Scottish Executive prior to 2007, is responsible in Scotland for all issues that are not explicitly reserved to the United Kingdom Parliament at Westminster by Schedule 5 of the *Scotland Act 1998*.

Devolved matters include health, education, justice, home affairs, rural affairs, economic development and transport.

The Scottish Government is led by a First Minister, nominated by the Scottish Parliament and by the Queen, who then appoints a Ministerial team, with the approval of Parliament, from the elected MSPs.

The Scottish Law Officers, the Lord Advocate and Solicitor General, can be appointed from outside the Parliament's membership, but are subject to its approval. The First Minister, the Cabinet Secretaries and the Scottish Law Officers are members of the Scottish Government. They are collectively known as the 'Scottish Ministers'.

Parliamentary elections in Scotland, initiated in 1999 when the Scottish Parliament was re-convened after a gap of almost 300 years, are held every four years. The current session which began in May 2011 will last for five years with the next election scheduled for 2016.

The First Minister appoints Cabinet Secretaries, including the Cabinet Secretary for Health, Wellbeing and Cities Strategy, whose responsibilities include:

'NHS, health service reform, allied healthcare services, acute and primary services, performance, quality and improvement framework, health promotion, sport, Commonwealth Games, public health, health improvement, pharmaceutical services, food safety and dentistry, community care, older people, mental health, learning disability, carers, Social Care and Social Work Improvement Scotland, substance misuse, social inclusion, equalities, anti-poverty measures, veterans, and cities strategy.'[1]

Role of the Health and Social Care Directorate

Within the Scottish Government the Health and Social Care Directorate is responsible for NHSScotland. The Director-General of Health and Social Care is also the chief executive of NHSScotland. As chief executive and accountable officer, this person is directly answerable to the Scottish Parliament for financial probity and regularity and for the economical, efficient and effective use of the resources allocated to the SEHD and to NHSScotland. In practice board chief executives report to the Director-General as the designated accountable officer for their board.

The Cabinet Secretary published the Scottish Government's strategy for a healthier Scotland in December 2007 – Better Health, Better Care.

In its leadership role, the Government issues detailed guidelines to assist in the implementation of policy objectives, and these can be accessed at the NHSScotland website. The Scottish Government's website for Health and Social Care is: www.scotland.gov.uk/Topics/Health

Role of regulatory/inspection agencies

For NHSScotland, the key regulatory and inspection bodies are:

- Auditor General/Audit Scotland: www.audit-scotland.gov.uk
- NHS Healthcare Improvement Scotland: www.healthcareimprovementscotland.org/home.aspx

You can find out more about these organisations at their websites.

---

[1] Source: www.scotland.gov.uk

Chapter 5: Organisational Structures: Running an NHS Organisation

The general principles of organisational structure as set out in chapter 5 are consistent with arrangements in Scotland. This includes roles and responsibilities of boards, chief executives, board members including non-executives and key committees.

One difference to note is that all appointments to NHS boards are made by the Cabinet Secretary. However the Scottish Government is currently conducting a pilot for the direct election of members to health boards in NHS Fife and NHS Dumfries and Galloway. This pilot will be formally evaluated before a decision is taken to extend direct elections.

The current structure of NHSScotland is shaped by a number of key reports including:

- *Rebuilding our National Health Service* (2001)
- *Partnership for Care – Scotland's Health White Paper* (2003)
- *Building a Health Service fit for the Future* (Kerr Report 2005)
- *Public Services Reform (Scotland) Act 2010.*

There are fourteen health boards and seven special health boards. Special health boards perform national functions – for example, Scottish Ambulance Service, NHS Education.

Rebuilding our National Health Service clarified the role of NHS boards as being strategic bodies accountable to the Scottish Government for their designated functions and the performance of the local NHS system.

There are no NHS trusts in Scotland, and there is comparatively limited use of the private sector in the provision of services.

In relation to specific committees, the background for NHSScotland is outlined below:

Audit committee

The 2004 *NHS Scotland Audit Committee Handbook* was replaced by the Scottish Government's *Audit Committee Handbook* in 2008. This applies to all bodies required to follow the Scottish Public Finance Manual, and this includes NHS Boards.

Clinical governance committee

A management executive letter, MEL (1998) 75, introduced clinical governance into the NHSScotland. Additional guidance has subsequently been issued including HDL (2001) 74 (which further clarified the need for clinical governance committees reporting to the board to be established with responsibility for oversight of the clinical governance arrangements) and MEL (2001) 29 (which further clarified the roles and responsibilities for clinical governance committees). *Rebuilding our National Health Service* defined two roles for this committee:

- systems assurance – to ensure that clinical governance mechanisms are in place and effective throughout the local NHS system

- public health governance – to ensure that the principles and standards of clinical governance are applied to health improvement activities.

Risk management committee

As noted in chapter 5, risk management committees are not mandatory however there is a need for assurance to be provided regarding the adequacy of risk management processes. Boards have discretion on how this is achieved. The publication of the *NHS QIS Standards for Clinical Governance and Risk Management* has led to some boards allocating this responsibility to the clinical governance committee. Other approaches involve risk management being explicitly reviewed by executive management groups or ensuring that the audit committee is kept aware of risk management activity and performance.

Staff governance committee

Rebuilding our National Health Service established that all boards must have a staff governance committee. This reflects the principle of partnership working (as evidenced by the requirement to have a staff member on NHS boards) and the recognition that staff governance is an integral part of performance management. Staff governance committees play an important role in ensuring consistency of policy and equity of treatment across NHS systems.

Service redesign committee

Partnership for Care: Scotland's Health White Paper established the need for boards to establish a service redesign committee to oversee the service improvement process. Service redesign committees promote the involvement of clinicians in planning and implementing improved services and are made up of a broad range of local clinical leaders.

Area clinical forum

The area clinical forum (ACF) consists of the chairs of each area professional committee. The chair of the ACF is a full member of the NHS board. The role of the ACF is consistent with the aim of involving clinical leaders in service planning, service redesign and co-ordinating the approach to clinical matters amongst the different professional groups.

Remuneration committee

A remuneration committee is a mandatory requirement. Duties are as described in chapter 5.

Research ethics committee

Health boards are required to have a research ethics committee. The principal function of this committee is to provide independent advice as to whether or not a given piece of research is ethical, and whether the dignity, rights, safety and well being of individual research subjects are adequately protected.

Directors of finance

This role is as described in chapter 5. Further details can be found in *Role of the Director of Finance* issued by NHSScotland Management Executive.

Chapter 6: Internal Systems and Processes: Statutory Requirements

Accountability

A *Code of Conduct for NHS Boards* was issued in 1994, which emphasises three crucial public service values, which must underpin the work of the health service. These values are accountability, probity and openness.

The basis on which NHS organisations in Scotland should seek to fulfil their duties and responsibilities is set out in the *Code of Accountability for NHS Boards* also issued in 1994 which included as one of its key objectives the need to 'ensure that high standards of corporate governance and personal behaviour are maintained in the conduct of the business of the whole organisation'. The Code also expands upon the role and responsibilities of the board, chairman, executive directors and non-executive directors.

Partnership for Care emphasised the need to devolve decision making power as far as possible to front line staff within an agreed framework of accountability for all staff. This should be achieved through a comprehensive scheme of delegation.

Priorities and planning framework

Since 2006/07 local delivery plans have been in place in Scotland and are effectively a delivery agreement between the Scottish Government and NHS boards, in the context of the national performance framework. Local delivery plans set out key objectives, targets and measures that reflect the Government's priorities. They also contain financial plans describing how the financial resources of the board are to be allocated to assist in the achievement of the key targets.

Alongside local delivery plans, NHS boards continue with planning arrangements at local and regional levels, engaging with local and regional partners across the full range of health policy, planning, service redesign and delivery issues.

With developments in healthcare generally (including increased specialisation amongst healthcare professionals) there is a need for a regional or national approach to the planning of services that need to be provided for populations greater than those of individual boards. HDL (2002) 10 created an explicit duty for boards to participate in effective and pro-active regional planning, and three regional planning boards now exist in NHS Scotland.

Standing orders and standing financial instructions

Standing orders (SOs), standing financial instructions (SFIs) and a scheme of delegation/ schedule of decisions reserved for the board are all required within NHS Scotland. The content of these documents is consistent with that outlined in chapter 6.

Accountability review

Formal accountability reviews will be held at least annually by the Cabinet Secretary using available performance information and including information from independent sources if available. The reviews result in feedback highlighting good practice as well as areas where improvement is required.

Annual accounts and annual reports

Again similar requirements for independently audited annual accounts and for bodies to prepare annual reports exist for NHS bodies in Scotland.

Chapter 7: Risk Management and the Assurance Framework

The statement on internal control

Statement on internal control (SIC) requirements as outlined in chapter 7 were introduced for NHSScotland through HDL (2002)11. The Scottish Government issues annual guidance on the sources of evidence and assurance which can be considered by a chief executive prior to preparing a SIC.

As the SIC requires a chief executive to report on internal control and risk management processes in place covering clinical, staff and financial governance, the chief executive will require evidence and assurance from the each of the staff governance, clinical governance and audit committees, as well as line management throughout the organisation.

The board's audit committee gathers these sources of assurance on behalf of the chief executive and the board, and considers them when reviewing the draft SIC and the annual accounts.

Risk management

Again the contents of chapter 7 are consistent with the position in Scotland. HDL (2002) 11 and the SIC require bodies to have risk management and review processes in place.

External audit

External audit is undertaken by Audit Scotland, which appoints private audit firms to deliver around a third of audits. External audit work is conducted in accordance with Audit Scotland's *Code of Audit Practice* and *Statement of Responsibilities of Auditors and Audited Bodies.*

Counter fraud services

NHSScotland Counter Fraud Services (CFS) provides a comprehensive and specialist counter fraud service to all of NHSScotland. All NHSScotland boards have entered into partnership agreements with CFS which include fraud action plans (these replace the previous fraud response plans). The aim of the partnership agreement is to reduce the risk of fraud through a pro-active and collaborative process involving both CFS and boards. To facilitate this process each board has appointed a counter fraud champion and a fraud liaison officer to work with CFS on all counter fraud work.

In 2005 the Scottish Executive built on the establishment of CFS and partnership agreements with the publication of the *NHS Scotland Strategy to Counter Fraud* within and against NHSScotland.

More details about CFS (including annual reports and the strategy) can be found at www.cfs.scot.nhs.uk

Chapter 8: Clinical Governance

Refer to comments on chapter 5, which outline the formal clinical governance requirements in Scotland.

Also note the role of NHS Healthcare Improvement Scotland in supporting quality – see its website for more details.

Chapter 9: Governance in NHS Foundation Trusts

There are no foundation trusts in Scotland.

Further reading

For details of the Acts referred to in this chapter visit: www.legislation.gov.uk/browse/scotland

Standards Commission for Scotland: www.standardscommissionscotland.org.uk/

For information about Best Value:
www.scotland.gov.uk/Topics/Government/Finance/spfm/BestValue

For information about Scotland's National Performance Framework:
www.scotland.gov.uk/About/purposestratobjs

Staff Governance Standard:
www.staffgovernance.scot.nhs.uk/what-is-staff-governance/staff-governance-standard/

Scottish Government: www.scotland.gov.uk/About/

Scottish Government's website for Health and Social Care: www.scotland.gov.uk/Topics/Health

Auditor General/Audit Scotland: www.audit-scotland.gov.uk

NHS Healthcare Improvement Scotland: www.healthcareimprovementscotland.org/home.aspx

For information about the NHS and healthcare in Scotland: www.show.scot.nhs.uk/index.aspx

Audit Committee Handbook, 2008: www.scotland.gov.uk/Publications/2008/08/08140346/0

For more about clinical governance (including NHS QIS Standards for Clinical Governance and Risk Management):
www.clinicalgovernance.scot.nhs.uk/section1/introduction.asp

Chapter 12: Governance in Wales

Chapters 1 and 2: What is Governance/ How the Elements of Governance fit together

The key underlying governance concepts set out in chapters 1 and 2 of this guide are equally relevant to NHS Wales. This chapter highlights key differences to indicate how these concepts have been taken forward in Wales.

Chapter 3: Public Sector Values and Organisational Culture

The broad principles outlined in chapter 3 apply in Wales. However, many of the codes of practice referred to (including the *Code of Conduct for NHS Managers* and the *NHS Constitution*) apply only to England.

In Wales, the key guidance in this area is the standards of good governance and in particular, the Welsh Government's *Citizen Centred Governance Principles*. These embody what the Welsh Government wants public services to be – namely 'focused on the needs of citizens, with citizens who are engaged and involved in the development of services and who receive services which are efficient, effective and innovative in their design and implementation'.

The principles are:

- putting the citizen first – putting the citizen at the heart of everything and focusing on their needs and experiences; making the organisation's purpose the delivery of a high quality service
- knowing who does what and why – making sure that everyone involved in the delivery chain understands each other's roles and responsibilities and how together they can deliver the best possible outcomes
- engaging with others – working in constructive partnerships to deliver the best outcome for the citizen
- living public sector values – being a value-driven organisation, rooted in Nolan principles and high standards of public life and behaviour, including openness, customer service standards, diversity and engaged leadership
- fostering innovative delivery – being creative and innovative in the delivery of public services – working from evidence, and taking managed risks to achieve better outcomes
- being a learning organisation – always learning and always improving service delivery
- achieving value for money – looking after taxpayers' resources properly, and using them carefully to deliver high quality, efficient services.

Chapter 4: The External Regulatory Framework

The role of Government

The Welsh Government has responsibility for health and social care in Wales. It comprises a cabinet of Welsh ministers led by the First Minister who is appointed by the Crown. Cabinet responsibility for the NHS in Wales rests with the Minister for Health and Social Services.

The National Assembly for Wales consists of 60 elected Assembly Members. It is the democratically elected body that represents the interests of Wales and its people, makes laws for Wales and holds the Welsh Government to account.

Detailed scrutiny of health matters is undertaken by the Assembly's Health and Social Care Committee.

Following the referendum held in March 2011, the National Assembly is able to create laws in all areas of devolved responsibility without the need to seek those powers from the UK Parliament.

Welsh Government Health and Social Services Portfolio

Minister for Health and Social Services

The Minister for Health and Social Services has responsibility and accountability to the National Assembly for Wales for the exercise of all the powers in the Health and Social Services portfolio.

National Advisory Board

The National Advisory Board is chaired by the Minister for Health and Social Services, and provides independent advice to the Minister. It assists in discharging ministerial functions, and meeting ministerial accountabilities for the performance of the NHS in Wales.

National Delivery Group

The Director General of Health and Social Services is responsible for providing the Minister with policy advice and for exercising strategic leadership and management of the NHS. The Director General is a member of the Welsh Government's Strategic Policy and Delivery Board, and is also the Chief Executive for NHS Wales. To support this role, he chairs a National Delivery Group, which forms part of the Health and Social Services Directorate General.

This group is responsible for overseeing the development and delivery of NHS services across Wales and for planning and performance management of the NHS on behalf of Welsh ministers. This is in accordance with the direction set by the Minister.

Health and Social Services Directorate General

The Health and Social Services Directorate General is the department that supports the Minister and the Director General in discharging their responsibilities. The Chief Medical Officer for Wales is also a member of the Health and Social Services Directorate General.

Programme for Government

The Welsh Government published their *Programme for Government* for the 4th Assembly to 2015 in September 2011. The *Programme for Government* sets out the specific actions the Government is taking, how it will judge whether these are on track and how it will assess progress in tackling the long-term challenges facing Wales. It is a working document. Annual updates will monitor the progress in delivering the programme. It includes sections on 21st century healthcare and supporting people, which cover the commitments for the Health and Social Services portfolio.

Role of regulatory/inspection agencies

For NHS Wales, the key regulatory and inspection bodies are:

- the Healthcare Inspectorate for Wales (HIW)
- the Wales Audit Office (WAO)

Healthcare Inspectorate Wales (HIW) is the independent inspectorate and regulator of all healthcare in Wales. HIW carries out its functions on behalf of Welsh ministers and protocols have been established to safeguard its operational autonomy.

Its primary focus is on:

- making a significant contribution to improving the safety and quality of healthcare services in Wales
- improving citizens' experience of healthcare in Wales whether as a patient, service user, carer, relative or employee
- strengthening the voice of patients and the public in the way health services are reviewed
- ensuring that timely, useful, accessible and relevant information about the safety and quality of healthcare in Wales is made available to all.

The WAO was created as a result of the merger of the Welsh element of the National Audit Office (NAO) and the Audit Commission in Wales.

National Assembly for Wales's Public Accounts Committee

The role of the Public Accounts Committee is to ensure that proper and thorough scrutiny is given to Welsh Government expenditure. The Committee will consider reports prepared by the Auditor General for Wales on the accounts of the Welsh Government and other public bodies, and on the economy, efficiency and effectiveness with which resources were employed in the discharge of public functions. Its remit also includes specific statutory powers under the *Government of Wales Act 2006* relating to the appointment of the Auditor General, his or her budget and the auditors of that office. It therefore plays a key role in scrutinising health service provision in Wales.

Chapter 5: Organisational Structures: Running an NHS Organisation

Organisation of the NHS in Wales

The NHS in Wales comprises seven health boards and three NHS trusts. Each health board has a unified allocation to fund healthcare for their population. The allocation for hospital and community health services is based on resident populations. Allocations for general medical services and prescribing are based on registered populations, and pharmacy and dental contract allocations are based on provision of services. Specialist services are planned and funded jointly by the health boards through the Welsh Health Specialised Services Committee.

Health boards

The seven health boards are single local health organisations that are responsible for delivering all healthcare services within a geographical area, rather than the trust and local health board system that existed previously.

The seven health boards are formally accountable to the Minister through the Chief Executive, NHS Wales. They are responsible for:

- planning, designing, developing and securing delivery of primary, community, secondary care services
- specialist and tertiary services for their areas, to meet identified local needs within the national policy and standards framework set out by the Minister.

The health boards adhere to the standards of good governance set for the NHS in Wales, which are based on the Welsh Government's *Citizen Centred Governance Principles*.

Health boards have a statutory financial duty to keep within their revenue and capital resource limits. In addition they are expected to achieve a 95% compliance rate with the *Better Payment Practice Code*.

NHS trusts

There are three NHS trusts in Wales:

- the Welsh Ambulance Services NHS Trust provides emergency and non-emergency ambulance services and manages NHS Direct in Wales
- Velindre NHS Trust provides specialist cancer services for South Wales, as well as hosting several all-Wales services, including the Welsh Blood Service and the NHS Wales Informatics Service
- Public Health Wales NHS Trust – provides all-Wales screening services and a National Public Health Service.

NHS trusts have a statutory duty to break-even, which is measured on an annual basis. They are also expected to keep within their capital resource limits and external financing limits and achieve a 95% compliance rate with the *Better Payment Practice Code*.

Appointment of board members

The Minister for Health and Social Services appoints the chair, vice-chair and non-officer members of local health boards (LHBs). The *Local Health Boards (Constitution, Membership and Procedures) (Wales) Regulations 2009* govern the appointment and removal of LHB board members. The *NHS Trust (Membership and Procedure) Regulations 1990* govern the appointment, and removal, of trust board members for Velindre and Welsh Ambulance Services NHS Trusts. The *Public Health Wales NHS Trust (Membership and Procedure) Regulations 2009* govern the arrangements for that organisation.

Local health board and NHS trust committees

LHBs and NHS trusts are required to establish a committee structure that it determines will best meets its own needs, taking account of any regulatory or Welsh Government requirements. As a minimum, LHBs must establish committees that cover the following aspects of board business:

- quality and safety
- audit
- information governance
- charitable funds
- remuneration and terms of service
- *Mental Health Act* requirements.

A *Governance Good Practice Guide* has been produced on effective board committees, which aims to provide advice on a range of issues surrounding the design, operation and development of board committees, within the following framework:

- why boards need committees
- what types of committees NHS boards need
- establishing committee arrangements
- making committees work for you
- evaluating and improving committees.

The guide also includes sample terms of reference for some of the key standing committees that may be established within NHS bodies.

The NHS Wales *Audit Committee Handbook* was updated in April 2011. A *Quality and Safety Committee Handbook* was issued in September 2011. Guidance on the establishment of other committees can be found on the NHS Wales Governance website.

Chief executive/accountable officer

In Wales it is the Chief Executive, NHS Wales who designates trust and LHB chief executives as accountable officers. Their duties are formalised in an *Accountable Officer Memorandum*.

Chapter 6: Internal Systems and Processes: Statutory Requirements

The principles set out in chapter 6 in relation to accountability, standing orders, the reservation and delegation of powers, annual accounts and annual reports are broadly consistent with Welsh arrangements. Wales's planning and priorities framework is outlined below.

Priorities and planning framework

Health and social care strategy in Wales – five-year Service, Workforce and Financial Strategic Framework for NHS Wales

Following the major reform of the structures of NHS Wales in 2008/09, a five year *Service, Workforce and Financial Strategic Framework* was commissioned. This Framework is designed as a flexible plan that can 'respond to the challenges faced by one of most complex organisations in the UK'. The overall aim is to 'improve health, raise system and service performance and quality, and transform health services and in turn transform people's lives.' This involves creating 'world class integrated health, social care and wellbeing services for the people of Wales, within five years, based firmly upon cross public service collaboration'.[1]

The Framework consists of a set of documents including the Welsh Government's 2010 document *Delivering a Five-Year Service, Workforce and Financial Strategic Framework for NHS Wales,* and the seven LHB delivery plans which will continue to be developed and refined year on year with partners. These plans will be populated with local service delivery priorities and also with best practice generated by eleven national programmes that form another part of the Framework. Other plans prepared with local partners will need to feed into this, particularly Community Strategies, Health Social Care and Well-Being Strategies and Children and Young People's Plans.

LHBs and local authorities have a duty to work in partnership to prepare and implement a 'health, social care and well-being strategy and a children's and young people's plan for their local area. The current plans cover the period 2011/12 to 2013/14.

Performance monitoring

The Health and Social Services Directorate General has issued an *Annual Quality Framework* for the NHS in Wales for 2011/12. This sets out the ministerial and other priorities that the NHS has to achieve in the year from within the revenue allocation. The Framework has been developed within the context of the *Five Year Strategic Framework*. NHS organisations are required to submit annual plans which set out in detail how they will deliver service improvements within available funding.

Performance management of NHS Wales organisations is undertaken by the Health and Social Services Directorate General, and follows six key principles:

- self-governance
- proportionality
- transparency
- openness
- minimal duplication
- minimal information.

---

[1] Health in Wales website: www.wales.nhs.uk/news/16445

The Directorate General is supported by a Delivery and Support Unit and the National Leadership and Innovation Agency in Healthcare in relation to performance management and improvement of NHS Wales organisations.

Chapter 7: Risk Management and the Assurance Framework

The assurance framework

Welsh health bodies are required to have a risk management framework that ensures a systematic approach to internal control. Organisations should ensure that they have evidence that they deem sufficient to demonstrate that they have implemented processes appropriate to their circumstances. The Welsh Government sets out in its framework *Putting Things Right* the importance of an integrated system of risk management to enable the effective management of risk.

Risk management

The Welsh Risk Pool (WRP – a mutual self insurance organisation that funds clinical negligence claims) plays a key role in supporting the development of risk management systems by providing advice, developing education in healthcare risk management and facilitating the exchange of information on good practice and lessons learnt through risk managers and claims managers' network.

Putting Things Right was established to review the existing processes for the raising, investigation of and learning from concerns. In this context, 'concerns' are issues identified from patient safety incidents; complaints and (in relation to Welsh NHS bodies) claims about services provided by a 'responsible body'in Wales. The aim is to provide a single, more integrated and supportive process for people to raise concerns which:

- is easier for people to access
- people can trust to deliver a fair outcome
- recognises a person's individual needs (language, support, etc.)
- is fair in the way it treats people and staff
- makes the best use of time and resources
- pitches investigations at the right level of detail for the issue being looked at
- can show that lessons have been learnt.

The Statement on Internal Control

All boards of NHS bodies, as part of their mandatory governance responsibilities, are required to conduct a review of the effectiveness of their systems of internal control at least annually.

The Statements on Internal Control (SICs) signed by accountable officers of Welsh health bodies form part of the assurance that informs the chief executive of NHS Wales's (the accounting officer's) SIC. The accounting officer's statement on behalf of NHS Wales in turn forms part of the assurance that informs the Welsh Government's SIC submitted to the Treasury.

Counter fraud and corruption work

Every NHS organisation is required to have a Local Counter Fraud Specialist (LCFS), under Welsh Government directions.

There should be mutual rights of access between the chair of the audit committee and the LCFS. There should also be an annual bilateral meeting between the chair of the audit committee and the LCFS to ensure that there is clear understanding of expectations and mutual understanding of current issues.

The Counter Fraud and Security Management Service carry out quality inspections of the whole NHS organisation's approach to countering fraud.

Chapter 8: Clinical Governance

In NHS Wales, clinical governance is not considered a separate requirement, but is a key element of a citizen centred governance framework. Quality and safety committees provide assurance to NHS Wales boards on the quality and safety of services they provide, plan and commission.

Chapter 9: Governance in NHS Foundation Trusts

There are no foundation trusts in Wales.

Further reading

NHS Wales Governance Manual (includes Citizen Centred Principles): www.nhswalesgovernance.com

Government of Wales Act 2006: www.opsi.gov.uk/acts/en2006/2006en32.htm

Welsh Government, Health and Social Care Department website: http://new.wales.gov.uk/topics/health/

NHS Wales website: www.wales.nhs.uk/index.cfm

The Healthcare Inspectorate for Wales (HIW): www.hiw.org.uk/

The Wales Audit Office (WAO): www.wao.gov.uk/

Welsh Risk Pool: www.wales.nhs.uk/sitesplus/955/page/52730

Appendix 1: Are our governance arrangements effective – a self assessment tool for boards

This appendix lists a series of questions that a board may wish to use as a self assessment tool to review the health of its organisation's governance framework. Each section is linked to a specific chapter of the guide so that background information can be accessed readily. Although the checklists cover all key governance issues, they are not designed to be exhaustive and boards should bear in mind their own local circumstances and concerns as they use them, amending or adding questions as they go.

	Questions for the board	Board response and supporting evidence	Action points
1.	How well do we understand what governance is all about (chapter 1)?		
1.1	Do new board members receive appropriate induction on appointment?		
1.2	Does this include awareness of the principles of good governance?		
1.3	Are all board members aware of the Nolan principles – do they adhere to them?		
1.4	Do board members understand what the organisation's primary purpose is – to provide a high quality, sustainable service?		
1.5	Do board members appreciate how wide ranging their responsibilities are?		
1.6	Does the board understand governance and why an integrated approach across all activities is important?		
1.7	Do members consider that they and the organisation generally comply with the principles of good governance?		
1.8	Does the board ensure that it is aware of lessons from governance failures both in the public and private sectors and is action taken in response when needed?		
2.	Do we understand how the elements of governance fit together (chapter 2)?		
2.1	Does the board appreciate that the organisation's tone is important and does it play a key role in its establishment and maintenance?		
2.2	Is the organisation's structure clear, and coherent?		

	Questions for the board	Board response and supporting evidence	Action points
2.3	Do board members understand how the structure fits together?		
2.4	Do board members understand how the organisation fits into the overall structure of the NHS?		
2.5	Do board members understand who is responsible for what within the overall organisational structure?		
2.6	Is there sufficient openness – from managers to the board and NEDs?		
2.7	Is there sufficient challenge at board meetings?		
2.8	Do we learn from our own and others' failures?		
2.9	Do we have a process for recovery if a governance breakdown occurs?		
3.	**Do we appreciate the importance of adhering to public sector values and have a distinctive organisational culture (chapter 3)?**		
3.1	Does the organisation have a distinctive ethos or culture? If so, is this widely shared among people within the organisation? How does the board confirm that this is the case in practice? Is this ethos consistent with the principles of good governance? If the answer to any of these questions is no, what is the board doing to address this?		
3.2	Does the board lead by example and set the organisation's overall tone and behavioural standards? If not how can this be achieved?		
3.3	Has the board developed a meaningful vision/values statement that is communicated to all staff?		
3.4	Do board members adhere to the Nolan principles and are they known, understood and applied throughout the organisation?		
3.5	Are board members aware of the principles and values of the *NHS Constitution*? Are they understood and accepted within the organisation? If so, are they applied in practice?		

	Questions for the board	Board response and supporting evidence	Action points
3.6	Are board members aware of the NHS *Codes of Conduct and Accountability* and the *Code of Practice on Openness* and are they followed?		
3.7	Are attitudes and behaviour within the organisation in accordance with all relevant NHS codes of practice/conduct? How does the board know that this is the case? What is the board doing to address any lack of awareness and compliance?		
3.8	Are all staff made aware of the *Code of Conduct for NHS Managers* and the need for compliance? If not how is the board planning to address this?		
3.9	Is the quality of leadership clear and effective throughout the organisation? How does the board know?		
3.10	Does the board review its own effectiveness every year?		
4.	**Do we understand how the organisation is affected by the external regulatory framework (chapter 4)?**		
4.1	Do we understand the role of the Secretary of State and Department of Health in relation to our organisation?		
4.2	(For FTs) do we understand the role of Monitor in relation to our organisation?		
4.3	(For NHS trusts and PCTs at present) do we understand the role of the Strategic Health Authority in relation to our organisation?		
4.4	(For PCTs prior to abolition) Do we understand our continuing legal responsibilities?		
4.5	Do we understand the role of the external auditors in relation to our organisation?		
4.6	Do we understand the role of the Care Quality Commission in relation to our organisation?		
4.7	(For PCTs prior to abolition) Do we understand how we hold the cluster management to account?		

	Questions for the board	Board response and supporting evidence	Action points
4.8	Do we as a board have sufficient assurance on the disclosures made to regulators?		
4.9	Are we well informed and updated on the reports issued by these bodies? Do we look out for learning points and act upon them?		
4.10	Does our organisation respond as we would wish to the requirements of these bodies?		
4.11	Do we, as a board, give sufficient time and consideration to the external auditor's reports on our organisation?		
4.12	Do all these external organisations understand our objectives and approach?		
5.	**Are our organisational structures fit for purpose (chapter 5)?**		
5.1	Did we receive induction that clearly set out the overall structure of the NHS from Parliament through to our own organisation and within our own organisation?		
5.2	Are we clear about our roles and responsibilities and those of our board committees?		
5.3	Do we review the committee structure regularly and ensure that each one adds value?		
5.4	Do we, as a board, fulfil the Higgs requirements of: • sharing collective responsibility for adding value to the organisation – promoting the organisation's success and directing and supervising its affairs • providing leadership within a framework of prudent and effective control which enables risk to be assessed and managed • looking ahead – setting the strategic vision and challenging/approving the aims/objectives set by the chief executive • setting and maintaining culture and values. If so, what evidence do we receive that we fulfil them all effectively? Are the organisation's outcomes what we intended and expected?		

	Questions for the board	Board response and supporting evidence	Action points
5.5	Do we, as a board foster and encourage constructive challenge?		
5.6	Do we understand the priorities facing the organisation and receive sufficient information in the right format and at the right time to make a judgement on the management of the agenda?		
5.7	Do we understand the distinctive roles and responsibilities of the organisation's audit committee, remuneration committee and (in the case of PCTs) professional executive committee? If so, do we receive effective advice and feedback from each committee?		
5.8	Are charitable funds managed by a dedicated committee that is NOT a board committee? Do we understand that charitable funds are separate from NHS monies and that they are governed by charity law and the Charity Commission's regulatory regime?		
5.9	Do we, as a board, feel that the chief executive: • helps us project a clear vision for the organisation • provides information and expertise to the board • provides operational leadership • provides effective control systems • delivers against operational objectives • delivers the modernisation and change agenda. If so, what evidence do we have that she/he does so effectively? Are the organisation's outcomes what we intended and expected?		
5.10	Do we, as a board: • challenge the vision and develop high level strategic objectives to achieve it • support the management of the organisation • set demanding but realisable operational objectives • challenge and thereby reinforce the effectiveness of control systems		

	Questions for the board	Board response and supporting evidence	Action points
	• support the chief executive in making changes and taking risks by corporately agreeing plans and strategies and taking corporate responsibility for outcomes • establish a forward thinking, modernising, high quality and patient-focused culture for the organisation. If so, what evidence do we have that we do all of these effectively? Which do we do best? Which do we do least well? Do we stray too far into areas that are management's responsibility?		
5.11	Do the organisation's structures and committees allow all important matters to be addressed at an appropriate level? Do we know what the appropriate levels are? What is the escalation process? Do committees tend to compartmentalise problems and decisions? Or do they enable all aspects of key issues to be taken into account in an integrated manner (for example, clinical, financial, structural etc.)? What examples do we have of decisions and plans that take effective account of all aspects? What examples do we have of poor decisions or plans, which did not take account of all aspects?		
5.12	Do we have clear structures, processes and accountabilities in place for partnership working? How do we assess their effectiveness?		
5.13	Do we have a clear understanding of governance arrangements for outsourced services? In particular do we know what risks the organisation has retained?		
6.	**Do our internal systems and processes meet statutory requirements (chapter 6)?**		
6.1	Are the roles of the chair and chief executive clearly distinguished and understood by board members? Are these roles respected by the incumbents? Do they fulfil their respective roles effectively?		
6.2	Do we have a 'job description' for the board and do we review our performance against it?		

	Questions for the board	Board response and supporting evidence	Action points
6.3	Do we clearly understand the powers and decisions that are reserved to the board? If so, do these include: • financial stewardship responsibilities, including adopting the annual report and accounts • determining the organisation's strategy and policies and setting its strategic direction • appointing senior executives • overseeing the delivery of services • standards of governance and behaviour		
6.4	Does the organisation maintain a meaningful set of standing orders, which is reviewed and renewed by the board on a regular basis? Do they facilitate the effective conduct of business by the board? Are all board members and staff aware of the SOs and are they adhered to? How do we test that this is the case?		
6.5	Does the organisation maintain a scheme of delegation, including powers reserved to the board, which is reviewed and renewed by the board on a regular basis? Does this facilitate the effective and appropriate conduct of business by the organisation? Are all board members and staff aware of the scheme and is it adhered to? How do we test that this is the case?		
6.6	Does the organisation maintain and regularly review its standing financial instructions? Are all board members and staff aware of the SFIs and are they adhered to? How do we test that this is the case?		
6.7	Does the board meet regularly? If so, does the frequency, format and approach of the meetings allow the board to 'retain full and effective control over the organisation'?		
6.8	Does each meeting receive a performance report, which provides an up to date progress report on key strategic objectives and risks previously identified by the board? Do board members have the opportunity to critically challenge the progress made and the evidence that supports it?		

	Questions for the board	Board response and supporting evidence	Action points
6.9	Does the organisation maintain an assurance framework? Is it fit for purpose and in line with the organisation's main objectives? How does the board use the AF? Is the guidance set out in the *Audit Committee Handbook* followed?		
6.10	Does the board discuss the organisation's operational plan at least annually? Does the organisation's plan meet NHS requirements in terms of structure and the priorities for action? How are we briefed on these requirements? Does the organisation's plan demonstrate measures that are realisable and affordable as well as indicate how these will meet national priorities?		
6.11	How do we ensure that we are aware of policy developments? Do we assess their impact on the organisation?		
6.12	Are we aware of the requirements and expectations of external bodies such as the CQC?		
6.13	How do we ensure that we meet our statutory duty to involve patients in service planning and proposals for change?		
6.14	Does the board devote sufficient time to reviewing the annual report and accounts, the quality account and the SIC?		
6.15	Do we have in place a whistle blowing policy that all staff know about?		
7.	**Do we have an effective approach to risk management and assurance (chapter 7)?**		
7.1	Do we understand what an assurance framework is for and how it is developed?		
7.2	Is our assurance framework clear and understandable?		
7.3	Are we involved in developing, reviewing and maintaining our assurance framework and do we use it to focus board discussions?		
7.4	Are performance management outcomes reflected within the assurance framework?		

	Questions for the board	Board response and supporting evidence	Action points
7.5	Do we understand the principal objectives in the assurance framework? Do we recognise them and was the board involved in establishing them?		
7.6	Have the principal risks been explained to us? Do we understand the controls which are expected to mitigate these?		
7.7	Do we understand the difference between risk management reports that focus on principal risks and those that identify significant potential risks for the assurance framework?		
7.8	Do we understand the sources of assurance and information we receive? What evidence do we have that these sources/information are reliable?		
7.9	Are the sources of assurance we receive sufficient?		
7.10	How do we know that the items reported to us cover all important issues?		
7.11	Do we receive routine performance reports for all activities? Are these clear and understood? Is the information that lies behind them reliable?		
7.12	Do we know how to differentiate between the value and relevance of sources of assurance?		
7.13	Do we know what to do when we receive negative assurances? Are we assured? Should we seek further assurances?		
7.14	What assurance do we have that emerging priorities are bought to our attention?		
7.15	How do we know if our audit committee (and any risk management committees) are effective?		
7.16	Are we familiar with the organisation's system of internal control? Are we able to assess whether or not gaps in control identified in the assurance framework cast doubt on the effectiveness of the overall system?		

	Questions for the board	Board response and supporting evidence	Action points
7.17	Are we asked to approve the action plans to address gaps in control and gaps in assurance? Do we receive clear and regular progress reports on these action plans? What assurance do we have that these plans are followed through to an effective outcome? Do we receive exception reports on items still outstanding?		
7.18	Is the board clear about what it has delegated and to whom?		
7.19	Has the concept of 'risk appetite' been discussed by the board? Have we been involved in agreeing the organisation's 'risk appetite'?		
7.20	Has the board agreed escalation procedures for risks? Are these procedures followed?		
7.21	Do we understand the organisation's risk management strategy? What evidence do we have that it covers all activities and objectives?		
7.22	Do we understand how the organisation's risk register is populated and how the principal risks are identified? Do we understand how the principal risks link to the assurance framework?		
7.23	Are the controls and processes described in the organisation's statement on internal control familiar to us? Does the chief executive provide the board with a full briefing on the system of internal control?		
7.24	Does the board receive summary reports of the results of internal audit work? Is this work well directed? Does it lead to effective remedial actions or change of practice where necessary?		
7.25	How does the board know if internal audit is effective/fit for purpose?		
7.26	Does the board receive summary reports on the work of the LCFS?		

	Questions for the board	Board response and supporting evidence	Action points
8.	**Do we pay enough attention to clinical governance (chapter 8)?**		
8.1	Do our organisation's governance principles and practices apply equally to the management of clinical activities, in practice?		
8.2	Does the organisation's assurance framework include strategic clinical objectives and the risks, controls and assurances relating to these?		
8.3	What evidence do we see that good clinical risk management is applied in our organisation?		
8.4	Does the board receive regular reports on the quality of clinical care (for example, services that are quick, easy to access and well organised and, above all, deliver effective outcomes)? Is the board involved in setting policy and monitoring performance in relation to quality of care?		
8.5	Does the board receive regular reports on patients' experience and patients' involvement (for example, how patients feel about the way they are treated and what would make things better? Are their preferences respected? Is there sufficient information and support?) Is the board involved in setting policy and monitoring performance in relation to both increasing patient involvement and measuring and improving patients' experience?		
8.6	What evidence do we have that there is openness in dealing with clinical incidents? Are lessons learnt from clinical incidents? Are these lessons shared with other disciplines? Are there organisation wide policies that are known and understood? Is the organisation proactive rather than reactive?		
8.7	Does the board receive summary reports of complaints and clinical negligence claims? Does the board identify and discuss common themes arising from these? How do these reports correlate to other risks/ performance issues?		

	Questions for the board	Board response and supporting evidence	Action points
8.8	Is there a culture of openness between clinicians and management throughout the organisation?		
8.9	How is the clinical audit plan developed? Does the clinical audit plan cover the right areas of clinical risk/clinical objectives? Do we receive summary reports of the nature and results of clinical audit work? Is this work well directed? Does it lead to remedial actions or change of practice where necessary?		
8.10	Does the board promptly discuss the results of national inquiries into clinical failings in other organisations? What evidence is provided of our organisation's status relative to the findings of these inquiries? Are appropriate actions to prevent similar occurrences decided and implemented?		
9.	**For foundation trusts ... are our governance arrangements in line with Monitor's requirements (chapter 9)?**		
9.1	Are we all aware of (and do we understand) our terms of authorisation?		
9.2	Do we meet all the disclosure requirements set out in our terms of authorisation?		
9.3	Do we engage with local communities to encourage membership? Is our membership representative? Do we review regularly our strategy in this area?		
9.4	Do the boards of directors and governors have a consensus view of each other's role?		
9.5	Do we understand the relationship between the board of directors and the board of governors?		
9.6	How effective is the communication between the board of directors and board of governors?		
9.7	Is our shared governance role effective? How do we know?		
9.8	Do we regularly review our conduct in relation to the FT Code of Governance?		

	Questions for the board	Board response and supporting evidence	Action points
9.9	How do we obtain the assurances necessary to enable us to sign the required self-certification returns?		
9.10	Are we confident of the process to appoint and remove the external auditor including the role of the audit committee and the board of governors?		

Appendix 2: UK Corporate Governance Code – main principles

Section A: Leadership

Every company should be headed by an effective board which is collectively responsible for the long-term success of the company.

There should be a clear division of responsibilities at the head of the company between the running of the board and the executive responsibility for the running of the company's business. No one individual should have unfettered powers of decision.

The chairman is responsible for leadership of the board and ensuring its effectiveness on all aspects of its role.

As part of their role as members of a unitary board, non-executive directors should constructively challenge and help develop proposals on strategy.

Section B: Effectiveness

The board and its committees should have the appropriate balance of skills, experience, independence and knowledge of the company to enable them to discharge their respective duties and responsibilities effectively.

There should be a formal, rigorous and transparent procedure for the appointment of new directors to the board.

All directors should be able to allocate sufficient time to the company to discharge their responsibilities effectively.

All directors should receive induction on joining the board and should regularly update and refresh their skills and knowledge.

The board should be supplied in a timely manner with information in a form and of a quality appropriate to enable it to discharge its duties.

The board should undertake a formal and rigorous annual evaluation of its own performance and that of its committees and individual directors.

All directors should be submitted for re-election at regular intervals, subject to continued satisfactory performance.

Section C: Accountability

The board should present a balanced and understandable assessment of the company's position and prospects.

The board is responsible for determining the nature and extent of the significant risks it is willing to take in achieving its strategic objectives. The board should maintain sound risk management and internal control systems.

The board should establish formal and transparent arrangements for considering how they should apply the corporate reporting and risk management and internal control principles and for maintaining an appropriate relationship with the company's auditor.

Section D: Remuneration

Levels of remuneration should be sufficient to attract, retain and motivate directors of the quality required to run the company successfully, but a company should avoid paying more than is necessary for this purpose. A significant proportion of executive directors' remuneration should be structured so as to link rewards to corporate and individual performance.

There should be a formal and transparent procedure for developing policy on executive remuneration and for fixing the remuneration packages of individual directors. No director should be involved in deciding his or her own remuneration.

Section E: Relations with Shareholders

There should be a dialogue with shareholders based on the mutual understanding of objectives. The board as a whole has responsibility for ensuring that a satisfactory dialogue with shareholders takes place.

The board should use the AGM to communicate with investors and to encourage their participation.

Source: Financial Reporting Council, UK Corporate Governance Code, 2010.

Appendix 3: Good Governance Institute Maturity Matrix

www.good-governance.org.uk	NHS Boards: Integrated Governance Ready Reckoner: The Good Governance Institute Self Assessment Maturity Matrix developed originally by John Bullivant, Michael Deighan and Andrew Corbett Nolan with Sheffield Teaching Hospitals NHS FT						NEW Version 8.2 11/08
Key Elements:	**Progress Levels:**						
	N O 1: Basic level – Principle Accepted	2: Basic level agreement of commitment and direction	3: Early progress in development	4: Firm progress in development	5: Results being achieved	6: Maturity – comprehensive assurance	7: Exemplar
1. Clarity of Purpose aligned to objectives and intent	N O National targets and local priorities agreed with stakeholders and plans in place	Purpose debated and agreed; priorities and drivers established	Purpose is affirmed in public and internal documents	Board has mechanism for adding and removing services and/or care settings	Evidence that national targets and local priorities are being met and strategy review in place	Annual debate on purpose and impact scheduled by Board in light of achievement of purpose in year	Success has allowed Trust/Board to redefine/extend its role
2. Strategic annual agenda cycle with all agendas integrated encompassing activity, resources and quality	N O Annual cycle of Board activity established	Board papers required to consider clinical, finance, HR, H&S etc. implications	Annual cycle of Board activity in place; reporting format and strategic prioritisation in place	Cycle of Business is tested for strategic balance	Agendas established but dynamic to changing priorities	Clarity of action and follow up in place. Improvement framework in place	Trust/Board is recognised for joined up decision taking and adding value
3. Integrated Assurance System in place	N O Board has understood and recognised role of assurance framework	Assurance Framework covers activity, quality and resources are aligned to targets, standards and local priorities	Control mechanisms in place for all elements of the Assurance Framework	Assurance Framework is focused on key business issues; operational risk is managed at point of delivery	High risk sensitivity demonstrated throughout Trust/Board	Annual audit of follow up of SUIs, complaints etc. Board assured Assurance Framework reflects priority issues	Board confident through evidence that it has assurance of all systems across the health economy

NHS Boards: Integrated Governance Ready Reckoner:
The Good Governance Institute Self Assessment Maturity Matrix developed originally by John Bullivant, Michael Deighan and Andrew Corbett Nolan with Sheffield Teaching Hospitals NHS FT

www.good-governance.org.uk

NEW Version 8.2 11/08

Key Elements:	N O	1: Basic level – Principle Accepted	2: Basic level agreement of commitment and direction	3: Early progress in development	4: Firm progress in development	5: Results being achieved	6: Maturity – comprehensive assurance	7: Exemplar
				Progress Levels:				
4. Decision taking supported by intelligent information	N O	Information requirements spelt out	Information processing and analysis focussed on priorities	Intelligent information for Boards, stakeholders and regulators	Boards take decisions based on evidence	Board agendas time reduced through improved use of information	Decision taking improved through timely information	Evidence-based decision taking in place
5. Streamlined committee structure; clear terms of reference and delegation; time limited	N O	Committee structure reviewed with expectation of minimum standing committees and time limited task groups	Plan for value added committee structure prepared	Streamlined committee structure in place with clear terms of reference and scheme of delegation and reporting	Committees contain work at devolved level – except where tolerances breached	Task groups come and go when done	Temporary committees/task groups report on progress and need for extension if necessary	Board has more time and energy for strategic decisions
6. Audit Committee strengthened to cover all governance issues	N O	Audit committee role developed to take on independent scrutiny function	All committees and senior staff recognise Audit Committee role	Workload and agendas for Audit Committee planned	Audit Committee workload and agendas under control. Internal and external auditors and advisors aligned to agenda and role	System overhauled and working	Committees reviewed and working effectively within scrutiny regime	Audit Committee recognised for key scrutiny role in clinical and financial areas

	N/O							
7. Appoint Board supports, eg Company Secretary AND Senior Independent Director (SID) to support Board, Committees and head compliance unit	N O	Company/ corporate secretary role or equivalent defined and located in organisation	Search for appropriate individuals from within outside organisation	Company/ corporate secretary appointed / trained assumes compliance unit role. SID in place	Co. Sec holds compliance and tracking role for all assurance issue of the board	Co. Sec has improved compliance and support to Board and committee	Company/ corporate secretary role reviewed for contribution to Board and its business	Company Secretary recognised as a voice of the organisation
8. Selection, development review of Board members	N O	Clarity of role and needs of NEDs and exec board members	Board induction process in place	Non Exec competences known and gaps identified, All Execs trained in Board role and corporacy	Exec contribution reviewed at least annually	Discussion is streamlined and supportive of purpose, assurance and strategic objectives	Clear corporate performance objectives of all directors reviewed by Chair and CEO in line with performance assessment system	Whole Board is recognised as adding value
9. Board etiquette agreed	N O	Board has discussed its values and the way it wants to work	Etiquette applied and tested	Etiquette agreed and board reviews performance after each meeting	Board reviews other boards ways of working	Board allows others to observe and challenge its ways of working	Board improves its working and values and etiquette reviewed annually	Board working recognised as best practice
10. Development of individual Executive Directors and NED/NOMs by the Trust/Board to ensure Board corporacy	N O	Training needs recognised and plan prepared	Board shows leadership through own development programme	Corporate development programme in place for directors – annual corporate review workshop established	Board runs scenario and practices business continuity planning	Board demonstrates use of business continuity planning in practice	Board fit for purpose, succession planning in place	Board members active in training and development of peers elsewhere

Developed by GGI under license from the Benchmarking Institute. Further copies available from john.bullivant@good-governance.org.uk

Appendix 4: Example Assurance Framework

This appendix contains an extract from a 'real life' framework that integrates performance and assurance and is in use in an NHS organisation. Please note, it is not designed to indicate best practice but simply to show what an assurance framework can look like. Other examples are included in the *Audit Committee Handbook*.

Integrated Performance and Assurance Framework – Quarter 1, 2011

Trust objective	Quarterly performance against objectives	On/off trajectory	BAF risk
1. Improve Patient Care, further improving safety, clinical outcomes and patient experience			Yes 1h(i)
Sub Objective:			
1c) Embed the principles of compassionate care across inner XXX hospital and community services through the XX Compassionate Care Partnership, as part of enhancing the overall patient experience	1c) Compassionate care update and pilot findings to TME in July and scheduled for the Quality Assurance Committee in September 2011		
1d) Improve the quality of information provided to patients and establish systematic mechanisms to obtain regular feedback from patients, staff and GPs	1d) QAC and TME updates on GP engagement plans during June and July. Inpatient survey and action plan to Board provides assurance of overall standards being maintained and improvement actions identified. Staff open meetings on Performing for Excellence and New Hospitals developments in Q1		
1e) Continue to improve the cleanliness of our hospitals	1e) Cleaning is monitored by xx, as well as by the infection control committee. The target remains to deliver compliance by end of July 2011. Trust cleaned areas and cleaned communal areas remain the challenge. Data on performance is now highly visible and the system of divisional support to underperforming areas is in place		
1f) Embed the outputs of the Outpatient Improvement Programme across the Trust	1f) Delivering outpatient transformation consistently across all services remains elusive. From Q3 a system of internal financial incentives and fines will be in place where minimum standards cannot be delivered. All clinic capacity changes ought to have been completed by end of June and around two-thirds of the standards are being met		
1g) Significantly reduce the rates of cancelled operations and cancelled clinics	1g) We are not succeeding in cutting cancelled operations. Q4 10-11 saw significant on-the-day improvements, which have not been maintained in April and May. Further focused attention is needed if we are to prospectively manage capacity in theatre, for equipment and for beds		
1h) Ensure the timely review and adoption of NPSA and NICE guidance	1h) Only 2 alerts remain outstanding for NPSA guidance. NICE guidance remains an issue and is being managed through Quality and Safety Standards Committee and divisional performance reviews		
1i) Agree priorities with stakeholders to develop our sites as health promoting hospitals	1i) A 'Strategy for Health Promoting Hospitals' framework has been produced and shared with stakeholders and used to inform and underpin merger proposals		

Principal risks	Current risk score	Key controls	Assurances on controls	Gaps in control/assurance	Target risk score
Description of risk	*Current risk score, and relevant CQC Essential Standard/ KLoE*	*Most significant controls/ systems in place to assist in securing delivery of objective and managing principal risks:*	*Does the available assurance [process outlined below] provide evidence that controls/systems, on which we are placing reliance, are effective?* *(Indicate if management, internal audit or independent assurance)*	*Where are we failing to a) put effective controls/systems in place? b) gain evidence that controls are effective*	*Target (by Q4 unless stated)*
1h(i) As a result of skills and capacity constraints, a failure to manage acutely ill patients in a consistent way at all sites and all times, could result in isolated incidents of delayed responses to deteriorating patients **Executive lead:** Chief Nurse and Medical Director **Subcommittee role:** Quality Assurance Committee	**Current risk – Quarter 1 risk score:** (5 × 2 = 10) [Outset risk: as above]	Role of matrons in routine ward reviews and identifying issues. Role of Outreach team to support management of acutely ill patients. Performing for Excellence review results in more band 6 nurses with required skills on wards	*Management:* Resus team carries out frequent audits Managing Acutely Ill Patients group reviews targeted work Reports to Quality and Safety Standards Committee and Quality Assurance Committee confirmed robust approach to addressing the issues	*Detail:* Ward round frequency remains variable across specialties *Action:* Review through consultant job planning and rota reviews	*Target: Q2 2011/12* 5 × 1 = 5
	Essential Standard/ALE KLoE: Datix ref: 1381	Data on inappropriate admissions to ITU Serious Incident reporting mechanisms		*Detail:* Clinical model results in outreach team not present on all sites 24 hours per day *Action:* Out of Hours rota and consultant job planning reviews led by the Medical Director seek to improve senior presence on wards and timeliness of medical responses	*Target: Q2 2011/12*

Integrated Performance and Assurance Framework – Quarter 1, 2011

Trust objective	Quarterly performance against objectives	On/off trajectory	BAF risk
2. Deliver in-year financial targets and develop a plan for long term financial stability			
Sub Objective:			
2a) Achieve key financial targets including 1% surplus, capital resource limit and level 3 financial risk rating (FRR).	2a) See Financial performance report for July 2011 for Q1 performance summary		Yes 2a(i)
2b) Complete the pay and workforce consultation and implement the new staffing structures, delivering in-year savings of £21 million	2b) *The first phase of the PfE workforce changes are nearing the end of implementation. A small number of compulsory and voluntary redundancies have been made, but the vast majority of at-risk staff have been placed in new roles within a reduced staffing establishment. The paybill impact of those changes are embedded within budgets and rely on continued work to cut out agency staffing and minimise use of bank staff – whilst retaining local autonomy over decision making, and, above all, safety at the frontline*		
2c) Deliver in-year non-pay savings of at least £5 million, maintaining enhanced non-pay controls and strengthening the clinical procurement group	2c) *The clinical procurement group continues to review tenders and areas of expenditure. Across pharmacy and supplies our savings plans exceed five million pounds. Delivery is tracked and reports through the bi-monthly PfE board*		
2d) Productivity – achieve improvements consistent with the PfE timelines – theatre utilisation of 90%, improved outpatients utilisation and inpatient length of stay in upper quartile	2d) *Substantial progress has been made in improving theatre utilisation and a small number of theatre lists have been removed from Q2, whilst maintaining activity. Bed reduction work to meet upper quartile length of stay is being executed more slowly than is necessary. The Executive will review the resource being deployed to this major change programme, which is central to the adoption of the new hospital as well as to our financial stability*		
2e) Create a 5 year financial plan that maps a path to long term financial viability	2e) *LTFM iterations reviewed by the Finance and Investment Committee during Q1.*		

Principal risks	Current risk score	Key controls	Assurances on controls	Gaps in control/assurance	Target risk score
Description of risk	*Current risk score, and relevant CQC Essential Standard/ KLoE*	*Most significant controls/ systems in place to assist in securing delivery of objective and managing principal risks:*	*Does the available assurance [process outlined below] provide evidence that controls/systems, on which we are placing reliance, are effective?* *(Indicate if management, internal audit or independent assurance)*	*Where are we failing to a) put effective controls/systems in place? b) gain evidence that controls are effective*	*Target (by Q4 unless stated)*
2a(i) As a result of competing major change programme priorities in 2011/12, the Trust fails to meet cost improvement plans as required to deliver an underlying cost base consistent with the long term financial model **Executive lead:** Chief Financial Officer **Subcommittee role:** Finance and Investment Committee	**Current risk: Quarter 1 risk score:** **(4 × 4 = 16)** *Outset risk (Jan 11) score:* *5 × 4 = 20* **Essential Standard/ALE KloE:** KLoE 3.1 *Datix ref: 859*	Monthly review of CAU/ departmental results and performance between Executive and Divisional Management. LTFM sets out medium and long term financial strategy Targeted measures including enhanced purchasing controls to manage spend	*Management assurance:* Divisional Performance Reviews and Finance and Investment Committee (FIC) detailed monitoring of financial management arrangements. Trust Board review of financial performance. *External assurance:* External Audit review of financial resilience and Value for Money opinion provides assurance *Management assurance:* Performing for Excellence programme, Trust Management Executive (TME) and FIC monitoring	*Detail:* Issues remain re: slow delivery of cost improvement plans. The financial control culture within the organisation not reached full maturity. *Action:* Establishment of non-recurrent reserves to mitigate in-year position. Ongoing financial training and development for budget holders and key spend decision makers	*Target Risk* $4 × 3 = 12$
				Target Q4 2011/12	

Budgets agreed at CAU level in 2011/12 to ensure greater organisational ownership and traction re: financial commitments going forward	*Management assurance:* TME oversight of business planning and related reporting to FIC. *Internal Audit assurance:* Performing for Excellence programme review in audit plan 2011/12	
SLAs agreed with commissioners provides assurance on activity and payment	*Management assurance:* FIC and Board reporting on income risks	*Green*